MW00425113

Mystic Street
Meditations on a Spiritual Path

Mystic Street

Meditations on a Spiritual Path

S. T. Georgiou

NOVALIS

© 2007 Novalis, Saint Paul University, Ottawa, Canada

Cover design: Dominique Pelland
Cover image: © iStock International Inc.
Layout: Pascale Turmel

Business Offices:

Novalis Publishing Inc.
10 Lower Spadina Avenue, Suite 400
Toronto, Ontario, Canada
M5V 2Z2

Novalis Publishing Inc.
4475 Frontenac Street
Montréal, Québec, Canada
H2H 2S2

Phone: 1-800-387-7164
Fax: 1-800-204-4140
E-mail: books@novalis.ca
www.novalis.ca

Library and Archives Canada Cataloguing in Publication

Georgiou, Steve Theodore
    Mystic Street : meditations on a spiritual path / S.T. Georgiou.

Includes bibliographical references.
ISBN 978-2-89507-902-6

    1. Spiritual life. 2. Meditations. I. Title.

BX383.G45 2007   204'.32   C2007-903219-2

Distributed in the United States by Twenty-Third Publications:
www.23rdpublications.com

Printed in Canada.

All rights reserved. No part of this publication may be reproduced, stored in
a retrieval system, or transmitted in any form, or by any means, electronic,
mechanical, photocopying, recording, or otherwise, without the written
permission of the publisher.

The Scripture quotations contained herein are from the Revised Standard
Version of the Bible, Cokesbury, 1952.

We acknowledge the financial support of the Government of Canada through
the Book Publishing Industry Development Program (BPIDP) for our
publishing activities.

5   4   3   2   1   11   10   09   08   07

For my mother, Anastasia,
who was the first to teach me that
life is a mystery, and is holy

CHRISTOPHER JOHN ROZALES, 2006.

A mystic is a person who is deeply aware of the powerful presence of the divine spirit: someone who seeks, above all, the knowledge and love of God, and who experiences to an extraordinary degree the profoundly mystical encounter with the energy of divine life. Mystics often perceive the presence of God throughout the world of nature and in all that is alive, leading to a transfiguration of the ordinary around them. However, the touch of God is most strongly felt deep within their own hearts.

Ursula King
Christian Mystics:
The Spiritual Heart of the Christian Tradition

In essence, I think that everyone is a mystic.
Everyone is a poet.
Everyone is a sharer in the divine light.

Robert Lax
When Prophecy Still Had a Voice:
The Letters of Thomas Merton and Robert Lax,
edited by Arthur Biddle

Love sees what is invisible.

Simone Weil
Waiting for God

Contents

Acknowledgments

Warm thanks are extended to the following individuals who helped make this book a reality: Dr. Jane Dillenberger, Professor Emeritus and founder of the Religion and Art program at the Graduate Theological Union, Berkeley; Br. Patrick Hart, O.C.S.O., Abbey of Gethsemani; Dr. Michael Morris, O.P., Dominican School of Philosophy and Theology, Berkeley, California; Kevin Burns and Anne Louise Mahoney of Novalis; Anastasia and Maria Georgiou; Christopher John Rozales; Donald Main; Jacqueline Chew; Anne Escrader; Kenneth O'Keefe; Linda Pitcher.

I also extend infinite gratitude to the late Robert Lax, without whom this book (as well as my Ph.D. in theology and creative work in religion and art) would not have been possible. Thank you, Bob, for opening your door to me that windy night on Patmos in May of 1993. Since we met, the Way has become increasingly luminous, and intensely real. I often think of your words; they come back to me like an echo:

> So let in the Light whenever, wherever you can. And after cultivating the glow for a while, let it go, let it flow, transmit

it, and you're sure to receive more along the Way. *Just keep on loving.* That's the bottom line, son. Everything is here because of Love. That's why we were created—to love! Love keeps things going now, and for forever. Love sets us out on our journey and ensures our safe return. Go with that Flow; keep pace with the lovebeats of the Heart.

Robert Lax,
The Way of the Dreamcatcher

To the Reader

Those familiar with Steve Georgiou's recent book, *The Way of the Dreamcatcher*, will know that it focuses on Robert Lax, the poet, hermit, and mystic whom Georgiou calls his mentor. Lax, the close friend of Thomas Merton, lived on the Greek isle of Patmos, where Georgiou encountered him in 1993. The author would return there numerous times to meet with Lax until the sage's death in 2000.

It may be said that *Mystic Street* continues where *The Way of the Dreamcatcher* left off. The book relates Georgiou's spiritual and contemplative experiences while earning his doctoral degree in Religion and Art at the Graduate Theological Union in Berkeley, California.

This delightful work progressively imparts a young Christian's interior journey; it is a wonderful, innovative blend of theocentric tradition and modern revelation. Positive and inspirational, these meditations demonstrate the power of grace in our everyday lives. As Georgiou relates, "Every street is 'Mystic Street.'"

Like *The Way of the Dreamcatcher*, this book is filled with prayer-ful simplicity; it is also subtly (and yet profoundly) sacramental. Answers to difficult spiritual questions are given with creative ease, and deep and holy truths are succinctly expressed through personal encounters and events that offer new insights about Lax.

Highly ecumenical and interfaith in its scope, *Mystic Street* should appeal to a wide range of readers, particularly those who sense the divine Presence active in the world. Indeed, while reading this book I was reminded of a passage in one of Lax's journals wherein he senses the Spirit of God moving in everyone he meets, in everything he sees:

> I walk across the bridge on Lake Lucerne and watch the people coming towards me.... A holy principle, holy spirit, a spirit of life dwells within and activates them all. They think of themselves as moving along on their own purposes, and they are. But something greater than all of them, than all of us, is the ultimate source of their movement (and of their pauses).*

Mystic Street illustrates how life is an experiential journey of faith which all of us live in God, each in our own unique way, providing we remain open to Him. Wholly life-affirming, this "storybook of the Spirit" gives light and hope in dark times, and helps us to embrace (and trust in) the Mystery of Love.

May this uplifting testament of Agape bring more peace, joy, and illumination into the lives of its readers.

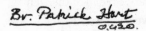

Br. Patrick Hart, O.C.S.O.
Last Secretary to Thomas Merton, General Editor of the Merton Journals, Abbey of Gethsemani, Kentucky, May 2007

---

*   Robert Lax. *Notes*. Zurich: Pendo-Verlag, 1981. 10.

Prologue

Earning a Ph.D. in theology is, to use a popular phrase coined by the Beatles, "a long and winding road." It involves specific language requirements, extensive classes and seminars, comprehensive exams, field research, teaching internships, and the culminating dissertation to write and defend.

In 2005, I completed my doctoral studies at the Graduate Theological Union (GTU) in Berkeley, an ecumenical and interfaith institution affiliated with the University of California. Nestled in the hills of a city widely known for its intellectual and artistic life, the GTU is recognized as one of the most prominent and interdisciplinary theological consortiums in the United States. The institution offers graduate programs in many diverse areas, ranging from the Cultural and Historical Study of Religions to Systematic and Philosophical Theology. My concentration was in Religion and Art.

While engaged in academic work, I increasingly began to see how spiritual study could also be undertaken *outside* of the classroom

Entranceway, St. Albert's Dominican Chapel, Oakland, California.

CHRISTOPHER JOHN ROZALES, 2006.

in an informal, natural, and almost spontaneous manner. What I mean to say is that I steadily came to apprehend traces of the spiritual in everyday life. In the subway, on the streets, walking to and from campus, talking with friends and faculty, deep insights were waiting to be discovered. A particular turn along a road, a conversation, the movement of people, even mere sounds could stimulate metaphysical reflection. Things visible seemed to lead to things invisible; valuable spiritual meditations could be cultivated through careful observation of day-to-day living.

The more I meditated on this idea, the more I saw points of revelatory interconnectedness in the people and environment around me. I took greater notice of "signs." For instance, why would a letter arrive from a friend on the very day I was thinking of that person? And how might a bird's flight relate to what I was feeling or where I was going? Surely if all of creation bears a common Origin, then strands of unity are threaded through every created thing; a kind of "spiritual string theory" may be said to run through the matrix of the cosmos, interconnecting life. Everything that exists intersects with all that Is; at any given moment, we have a type of communal access to the whole of things. This access can be intensely perceived through theocentric living, contemplation and prayer, intuition, dreams, and the psychic apprehension of the holy energies coursing through life.

Shortly after I began my doctoral studies, I happened across a street named *Mystic*, a simple though beautiful lane lined with maple and gingko trees whose leaves turned red-gold in autumn. I came to take this scenic path regularly en route to St. Albert's Dominican Priory and Chapel where I attended evening Mass and afterward received scholastic direction from my graduate adviser.

At first, "Mystic Street" seemed a Berkeley novelty, aptly named because of the theological activity in the area. But as time passed, I began to see how everyone is already living on "Mystic Street." From the Great Mystery of God we came, in the Presence of that Great Mystery we are, and into the Great Mystery we are returning. We are co-participants, fellow mystics in the divine life, and in grace. As such, we understand that everything we do has both literal and allegorical meaning; our lives are constantly conducted on an actual-symbolic, physical-metaphysical, natural-supernatural plane.[1]

The everyday act of opening a door demonstrates this reality. Opening a door is first of all a physical act, routinely and almost mindlessly done. Yet if we move through a portal gently, sensitively, aware that we are bringing something new into the room we enter (all the while conscious that whoever is in the room is, in turn, bringing something new to us), then a simple, everyday act comes to take on higher meaning. "Opening a door" becomes a metaphysical experience.

With this kind of awareness, we live knowing that there is something more to life than meets the eye, and so are awake to both the outer nature of things and the inner vision, to both seen and unseen possibilities, and to their interrelated harmony in divine Agape. Hence the Nicene Creed of the early Church states, "I believe in all things *visible and invisible.*"

This book is a collection of spiritual reflections I experienced while undertaking doctoral studies in theology. The meditations, loosely arranged over a seven-year period and presented in narrative and anecdotal form, were generated through scenes observed, situations and encounters, signs, symbols, fortuitous events, and dreams. Of varying length, the chapters range from "heavy" to "light"; some are deep, while others are quaint, even whimsical. Taken in its entirety, this book is an inward, contemplative journey of enlightenment, an intuitive (and experiential) way of sensing the divine Mystery at work and play in the cosmos.

The events and reflections described in these vignettes considerably strengthened my faith in the God of Love and helped me to complete the rigorous journey through doctoral school. Their positive, upbeat nature testifies to the workings of Agape in a world that some may feel has grown cold, cynical, hollow, empty of transcendent experience and revelation.

Though the inspiration for these meditations was originally conceived when I discovered "Mystic Street," the fact remains that every street is Mystic Street. Every lane we walk and every turn around every bend is an invitation to spiritual discovery. On Mystic Street, new insights about our relationship with the Creator and the cosmos are always possible. We have only to remain open to the understanding that the divine blessings of love and grace are unlimited, are unconditional, and are everywhere.

In essence, we live and move along avenues of potential awakening; we meet at intersections of enlightenment. As the pre-Socratic philosopher Empedocles said, "The nature of God is a circle, of which the center is everywhere and the circumference is nowhere."[2]

In that sacred Circle, anything can happen, because the Divine Mystery is both in all and beyond all. Thus Jesus exclaimed, "In God, *everything is possible*" (Matthew 19.26). Almighty Love is everywhere we are.

S.T. Georgiou
San Francisco
March 2007

Mysterious.
Life
is
consistently
mysterious.
A
sacred mystery,
a
journey…
A
story
of
faith and wonder,
a
prayer
of
light and hope;
a
never-ending
gift
of
love.

Robert Lax,
from a conversation
with the author,
arranged into verse form,
October, 1999

S.T. GEORGIOU, 1995.

The holy isle of Patmos with the town of Chora rising in the distance. In the centre looms the Byzantine Monastery of St. John. The monastery, erected on a high peak overlooking the sea, has beckoned many travellers through the centuries.

Walking on Water

Sometimes things work out all by themselves—or, as those who have faith in a higher power might say, through grace. How I found myself completing a doctorate in theology is a case in point. I really had no intention of re-entering graduate school, having already received a Master of Arts in the Humanities from San Francisco State University; I simply wanted to teach at local community colleges and eventually settle into a full-time post.

In 1993, however, I narrowly missed a prestigious tenure track appointment and, shortly thereafter, broke up with my girl-friend. These stressful events impelled me to leave everything behind and journey to the remote Greek isle of Patmos to experience some type of rejuvenation. Little did I know that the long road leading to my Ph.D. would begin at this distant locale.

But why Patmos? For about a year I had been writing to a monk there who suggested that the island would make for a good spiritual retreat. The Monastery of St. John the Theologian, erected on a high peak overlooking the sea, seemed to mystically beckon.

The isle is famous for its link with the Revelation (also known as the Apocalypse), as well as for miracles that are said to take place there. Empty as I felt, something told me that if I trusted in Providence and journeyed to the "Jerusalem of the Aegean," if I made the honest effort, things would steadily get better. Patmos seemed to be the ideal site for spiritual renewal, especially since Greek Orthodoxy, the religion of my birth, flourishes there.[3]

In late May I boarded a plane for Athens, and then took the ferry to this sacred place. After twelve hours on the sea, the dark mass of Patmos at last took shape against the night sky. The spotlights of the far-off monastery twinkled like stars as the ship slowly circled the craggy isle.

At about midnight, the vessel passed a great promontory. The hulk of rock slipped by silently, almost eerily, and then, all at once, the sweeping radiance of the main port streamed into view.

Something powerful was here for me, something salvific—I felt this sensation intensely. While most of the passengers bustled into town, I quietly made my way over to the nearby shoreline and sat in the sand, mystified by the pervasive presence of the Holy.

It was on Patmos where I met the man who would become my spiritual mentor and whose inspirational life and counsel would set into motion my theology program. Strangely enough, he was not a Greek monk, but Robert Lax, a Catholic hermit-poet and the best friend of the renowned Trappist Thomas Merton. Born in New York, he held a variety of odd jobs and travelled extensively until an icon he saw in Marseilles (of St. John writing the Revelation) prompted him to journey to Patmos in

1964. Lax soon made the hallowed isle his creative and spiritual workshop, residing there until his death in 2000. Though at first I knew nothing of the reclusive poet, I would eventually write a book on my experiences with Lax entitled *The Way of the Dreamcatcher*.[4]

So it happened that shortly after my arrival, I was pointed in the eremitic writer's direction by a young Greek who thought I could learn something from this man "Pax." As I would discover, he had Lax's name wrong, but somehow it was right, since I had come to Patmos to find "Pax," or peace.

In the course of our initial conversation, the tall, lean, white-bearded poet learned that I had written my Master's thesis on St. Augustine and had a fondness for poetry and icons. He consequently hinted that it would be worthwhile for me to augment my humanities interests, particularly in spirituality and the arts. When I returned home to California, I mulled it over for a year. Then, in 1995, I decided to travel back to Patmos and continue my discussion with Lax about this and other topics.

Amazingly, soon after my boat docked at the holy isle, I met a number of professors from the Graduate Theological Union in Berkeley, among them Sandra Schneiders and Robert Smith, both distinguished experts on Christian spirituality. I overheard them talking about Berkeley, and was intrigued. After mutual introductions, they encouraged me to visit the GTU (popularly known as "Holy Hill") and pursue theological studies there. It would turn out that I had journeyed 5,000 miles to attend graduate school just across the San Francisco Bay!

Yet when I eventually enrolled at the GTU, I was not sure exactly what it was I had come to learn. I had a wide variety of spiritual interests, and remained uncertain about specializing in any particular area. I only sensed that the campus had a warm and promising feeling, like Patmos, so I began taking classes, trusting that, in time, I would find a more concentrated academic path. Eventually, I completed a Master's in Theology and then, on the recommendation of my academic adviser, entered the Religion and Art Ph.D. program. Most fittingly, my doctoral work came to focus on the individual who had steered me right in the first place—Robert Lax. The result was a dissertation on the spiritual analysis of his poetry.[5] In full-circle fashion, the end of my graduate school experiences in theology happily joined with their beginning.

In retrospect, what I find interesting in all of this is that I did not consciously seek out any of it; I was simply responding to things that were coming my way, with trust. I had never intended to meet Lax, nor enter the GTU, nor acquire a doctoral degree in theology, yet gradually it became manifest, and simply because—as Robert Lax might have said—I "went with the flow." Despite ups and downs, I had an overall faith in where life was taking me.

Here the famous Arthurian tale of the sword and the stone comes to mind. Many powerful knights had come with great intent to draw Excalibur out of the stone and become king. But the boy Arthur, in all his youthful innocence, simply happened to come across the sword as he was walking through the forest. Intrigued by the luminous metal, he drew the blade out of the rock as naturally as one might lift a glistening shell from the sand. There was no self-centred intention—simply wonder and the purity of innocent belief and action.

This is how life itself is best experienced: through the simple belief and faith that eventually everything will turn out well according to the Wisdom from which creation issued and toward which creation is flowing. Little by little, things will come together, as long as one remains relaxed in the moment and lives "like a lily of the field" (Luke 12.27), unburdened by temporal concerns and fleeting, self-centred desires. Ultimately, this is how we draw near to the Creator and enter heaven; we shall inherit the kingdom if our hearts are gentle and unassuming, and we are as trusting and spontaneously loving as children (Mark 10.15).

A marvellous photograph of Simone Weil, a great religious thinker of the twentieth century, shows her in uniform during the Spanish Civil War. She found divine love amid much suffering, yet one would never know it from the snapshot. She appears serene, far from the world, as if God has called her name, and she hearkens to his voice. Somehow she stands outside of her earthly surroundings because she sees a greater Path. Trusting in a transcendent Power, she almost floats. Love has replaced doubt and fear; she has learned the secret of walking on water.

When the disciple Peter stepped over the waves in order to reach his Master, but then in fright began to sink, Jesus cried out to him in a loud voice, "O man of little faith, why did you doubt?" (Matthew 14.31). Like Peter, we are all called to trust in the Love that will carry us through the light and darkness of this life, and into the boundless radiance of the next.

Castle in the Sky

I would regularly return to Patmos during my graduate studies to learn more from Robert Lax and conduct research on my dissertation. It happened that during one of my summer trips, I decided to take the bus up to the medieval Monastery of St. John, the great mountaintop bastion that is fashioned like a castle in the sky. When I visited the monastery I would usually walk up from Skala, the main coastal town, but because of the intense heat during this particular day, I opted for public transport.

The bus was filled with local schoolchildren and a few chaperones who were on a field trip to the monastery. I moved to disembark, but the driver quickly assured me that it would be fine if I rode along, since he had heard that the next bus would be late in arriving. Gratefully, I took a seat toward the back of the vehicle.

While waiting for the bus to depart, the group's stern-faced leader briskly came down the aisle, collecting fares from the children. All had their money in hand and were prepared to buy a ticket. But one young girl, about eight or nine years old, seemed to have forgotten her cash. Almost immediately, her unsympathetic neighbours began taunting her, ridiculing her for her forgetfulness, impressing upon her that she would not be able to go to the "castle" (the monastery) if she had no drachmas forthcoming. I was sitting just across from her and saw how devastated and frightened she had become, thinking that she would be left behind.

As the group leader approached, the girl's schoolmates were eagerly talking among themselves, waiting for the moment when he would attempt to collect the child's nonexistent fare. She began to cry softly and crumpled up in a ball on her seat.

All at once I realized that I could help her—there were drachmas in my pocket doing absolutely nothing! I fished for the right change, reached over, and gave her what she needed to continue her journey.

Suddenly there was a holy stillness. We shared a suspended moment filled with awe, compassion, and heartfelt thankfulness. Her wide eyes repeatedly asked, "Why did you do this? You don't know me, and yet you saved me!"

Certainly it was a straightforward and mechanical gesture on my part, but to her it meant the world. Meanwhile, the children around her quieted to a hush, realizing that their unkind expectations had been foiled. A few looked away in obvious embarrassment.

In many ways, we are all like that child wishing to travel to "the castle" (home, heaven, a joyously collective and communally blessed destination), but have not the entire means to make it happen. We need the support, prayers, and assistance of our neighbours. We are created to help one another, to share with each other so that we might complete the journey of life together, that no one be left behind.

When I returned to San Francisco and regularly rode the subway to campus, this encounter often came to mind. Even now, when I take public transit, I occasionally think about it, for we are all on the same train, on the way to a similar destination. If life is a ticket to ride, then let us ride in the unity and solidarity of love. Who knows what happiness a smile to a fellow passenger or a silent prayer directed toward one's neighbour might generate? People intuitively know when they are loved, and when they are not. We are travellers of the heart.

S.T. GEORGIOU, 1999.

The 11th-century Monastery of St. John with surrounding homes. Patmos, Greece.

Subway Mysticism

"Subway Mysticism" is a phrase invented by Robert Lax and his lifelong friend Thomas Merton, monk, author, peace activist, and interfaith proponent. In their early 20s, these two gifted college students rode the New York transit system up and down Manhattan from Columbia University. To pass their time, they would feign trance-like poses and postures; as the train picked up speed, they would become completely still and close their eyes or would perform various *mudras* (symbolic Buddhist hand gestures) and physically assume the likeness of what they deemed to be illuminated yogis. In essence, the imaginative riders made it seem as if they were entering states of deep meditation and enlightenment while the train hurtled through the darkness and continued its reverberating subterranean passage.

Subway Mysticism was essentially a zany game designed by Lax and Merton for sheer amusement. After learning of their unusual pastime, I began thinking more seriously about how the subway commute could indeed be experienced in mystical fashion and could inspire spiritual contemplation. For a while, I kept track of

my railway meditations while commuting to and from campus.
During one particular ride I recorded this entry:

> The system is a vast network, running in and out of many
> cities and counties. Miles of track go down deep into the
> earth, then suddenly surface like rivers or land fissures

CHRISTOPHER JOHN ROZALES, 2006.

Balboa Station, a part of the Bay Area Rapid Transit subway system.

weaving their way up from the underground. This sprawling metromatrix, with its maze of tubes and tunnels, may be seen as a techno-extension of the human nervous system.

Electronic "nerve pathways" have been wired above and below. The winding, far-reaching railway hearkens of neuron circuitry. Thus when we stream through this "intelligent design," we are figuratively coursing through the voltaic channels of a greater Mind—a luminous and collective Consciousness, of which we are a reflective part.

Everyone in this synaptic grid becomes a unique idea in transit, en route to be realized. At an abstracted level, we are like thoughts participating in some progressive universal revelation, sparks firing and flowing toward some imminent Awakening...

My railway ruminations were considerably strengthened after visiting the Robert Lax Archives at St. Bonaventure, New York, where I gathered material for my dissertation. On entering the office of Paul Spaeth, Archive Director, I noticed a stack of Lax's handwritten notebooks sitting on the desk. In an almost reverent manner, I picked one up, opened it, and immediately turned to the phrase that I had entertained in my mind for some time: *Subway Mysticism.*

This uncanny coincidence was one of many that I experienced throughout my years of graduate school, and which began when I journeyed to Patmos and fortuitously met Lax. Exactly why these serendipitous occurrences took place I cannot say—perhaps some type of spiritual rejuvenation or reconnection was initiated when I came to the holy isle. I had, after all, arrived in an intensely desperate state, nearly broken in spirit, having almost lost faith in love and in the possibility of finding lasting joy in life. My flight to Patmos was like a last chance to live. Perhaps I was so empty that something beyond my knowing—in essence, the mercy of God—reached out of the great Infinity, infusing me with hope through periodic signs and seemingly coincidental encounters. Certainly meeting Lax was the most profound of these events. It seemed to have set everything into motion, catalyzing a profound spiritual relationship with him that would continue long after my last visit to Patmos in 1999, and even after Lax's passing in 2000. As he once told me, "We'll always be walking and talking together."[6]

Of course, travel to faraway places and meetings with wise elders are not necessary to experience the mercy and grace of God—our Father's life-sustaining and interceding Energy is operating here and now. All of us have immediate access to it because in this very moment we are alive in it; Mystic Street is everywhere. We only need to become patient (and quiet) enough to sense more keenly the gentle, loving Power that nurtures all things uniquely. If we do so, incidences that we might deem extraordinary would turn out to be increasingly ordinary, simply because our psychic receptors would be set at a higher frequency—the frequency of Agape.

While it is true that sometimes an illuminating journey is necessary to fine-tune our spiritual reception (be it a trek to Patmos or to a nearby park), the fact remains that the searcher ultimately discovers what was already within his or her possession from the very beginning: the transformative love of God, and the unceasing life of renewal in the Almighty. As Taoist philosophy relates, "Without leaving his door, the sage knows everything under heaven."[7] This process of inner spiritual rediscovery brings to mind the Tibetan story of the crow which, although already in possession of a pond, flew elsewhere to quench its thirst, but on finding no other adequate drinking place, returned to its own pond.[8]

Our life in God's constant love and grace is like riding the subway. Everything we need is already on the train, and we are heading for an infinitely blessed destination. It is up to us whether we stay on board (even when the ride gets bumpy) or get off.

My mentor thought it was wise to take it easy while in transit. Happiness, he would say, has a lot to do with finding a place of consistent rest, a place free from worry and anxiety and the stressful fluctuations of gain and loss. "Just sit back and relax," he would tell me, in his good-natured, easygoing fashion, "and you can journey anywhere."

The poet-hermit Robert Lax and Steve Georgiou at the waterfront in Patmos (1993). In *The Seven Storey Mountain,* Thomas Merton had said of Lax, "The secret of his constant solidity has always been a kind of inborn direction to the living God ... Lax was much wiser than I, and had clearer vision, and was, in fact, corresponding much more truly to the grace of God than I ..."

PANTELIS KLEIDIS, 1993.

Light Speed

Monday morning, the start of a new workweek. Spring day, clear blue skies. Sunlight pours onto the subway platform through the open steel canopy above. Everything is shining. An invigorating nip is in the air, a crispness that inspires activity. People are on the move, nearly all bound for work or school, and I am among them, headed for class.

Pigeons flutter through the golden morning rays; their falling feathers float and hover over the tracks like alighting angels. I look to see if anyone notices, but most commuters seem caught up in their own thoughts, or are listening to their iPods, talking into cell phones, or staring at their feet, which they shuffle restlessly as they wait for the incoming train.

As I stand at the front of the line, I glance at the yellow rubber matting covering the tiles closest to the tracks. The word *Pathfinder* is embossed on the raised, corrugated rubber—most apt, considering we find our way through the course of each daily commute.

A steady rumble indicates an approaching train. Its piercing light flickers in the distance and emerges out of the tubular darkness. Everyone comes to attention as the station bell sounds and the car streams into view, a silver blur sounding its horn until it gradually slows to a stop. The bird feathers, long since fallen to the tracks, are now flying toward the sky.

The metallic blue doors bolt open. Only a handful of people disembark, since most riders are headed for downtown and the East Bay. I cross the boarding threshold and at last stream into the thick of the metro current.

It is a new train. The clean, carpeted floors and blue upholstered seats complement the white fluorescent interior. Ads line the walls of the car. One, designed to increase enrollment at a local college, reads, "In ten years you will be …?"

I take an inside seat midway down the aisle. Commuters rush to come on board, but every seat is now taken. Standing, people grasp metal bars overhead and jostle for elbow room. Some position their travel bags to create more space for themselves—territorialism prevails.

Through the tall window panels I see a wave of last-second riders running to catch the train, but they are too late. A warning bell sounds. The doors close. An electric buzz whirs and increases in intensity.

Suddenly we are in motion. From a slow roll our speed increases and builds to a high-pitched electroglide hum. The train is now fast-tracking its way through the underground.

The railcar speeds on, gliding into station after station, relentlessly sounding its horn at each stop. At each consequent departure, the train slowly pulls away with a low rumbling moan, as if reluctant to leave. But within seconds the moan transforms into a rattle and then a roar and we continue to make our way down the long city run, then on to Oakland and Berkeley.

I listen to the tones of the train. As we travel, a constant hum rises and falls in hypnotic fashion. Sometimes I hear what seems like water rushing over stones, followed by a momentary deep bubbling, something like a scuba diver's underwater exhalations. But this quickly fades as other sounds come into play, tones that surge, crest, then ripple away as the electric current propels the coach onward.

Embarcadero Station: the last San Francisco stop. Directly ahead is four miles of tunnel, the Trans-Bay Tube, which dips down 135 feet underwater and connects San Francisco to Oakland. Every day, nearly 190,000 commuters hurtle through the tunnel at a maximum speed of 80 miles per hour. Though built over 30 years ago, the tube still remains a technological marvel, designed to shift slightly beneath the sea floor in case of a severe earthquake.

The railcar pulls forward. No matter how many times a rider has experienced the trans-bay railway commute, there is always a heightened sense of expectancy on entering the tube. At first one hears a low rumble, then what sounds like a shifting of gears. A sudden coolness pervades the air, and then the train slowly and almost imperceptibly descends beneath the bay, quickly gathering speed as it streams through the concrete and steel artery linking shore to shore.

We are submerged, going deeper, faster. Water pressure outside increases, though we are safe in this enclosed, fluid place. That we are travelling many fathoms beneath the water's surface and shall soon stream above ground distinctly hearkens of baptism, spiritual rebirth. We descend into the tunnelled depths and will eventually issue out of the tube on an inclined track that arcs skyward. From the bottom of the bay we shall ascend to the heights; emerging from darkness, we will bolt from the tunnel and enter the light. All at once the rays of the morning sun will flood through the full-length windows, illuminating the passengers and interior.

But now the railcar hurtles through the dark, roaring relentlessly over the tracks. The tunnel lights whiz past like comets or shooting stars. Already we are halfway across. One thousand DC volts of current propel the coach onward. Within moments we shall have reached maximum speed. Some riders repeatedly pop their ears to ease the mounting pressure. Those who are standing grasp the overhead bar tighter.

I think of the young Merton and Lax assuming trance-like states and meditative postures as their subway train reached top speed. They were playing a novel game, feigning enlightenment while caught up in the "velocity of illumination," but in a metaphysical sense, were the imaginative riders onto something? What does the speed at which we travel ultimately tell us? Where does it take us? How does it augment our ideas about where we are, and where we are going?

The very reason why I am aboard this train is to reach a destination. I have entered a pre-existent current of travel, am flowing with it, and thrilling to the supercharged speed of the journey.

The sheer velocity has set my awareness of life keenly on edge. I feel the immediacy of things building and am expecting some kind of change or breakthrough. In pushing the limits, the walls of one's living space give way, but to what? What kind of hyperspace am I on the verge of entering?

Quite possibly, it is the space of stillness. Paradoxically, we strive to go faster in order to stand still; when starting and end points meet, there is no further need for movement, because we have arrived. So the drive for ultimate speed seems deeply rooted in the inborn desire to be everywhere at once, instantaneously present throughout the cosmos, and this can only be mystically accomplished in God, who is All, in All. As St. Augustine stated throughout his *Confessions*, our incessant straining and striving is directed toward finding eternal peace in our Maker.[9] Speed may thus be seen as a subliminal quest for a higher power, which explains why Lax and Merton entered "enlightened states" when the train they were riding acutely accelerated.

Yet how exactly to meld with the Power that is everywhere at once? I remember Robert Lax asking me, "What particular button when pressed, can emit (and answer) all messages instantly?" Surely this "button," which everyone has access to, is prayer; it is the loving, boundless energy that immediately connects us with Creator and creation. St. John Chrysostom said it best: "Prayer annihilates the distances."[10] In prayer we literally travel at the speed of Light, and beyond. Or, as Thomas Merton put it:

> In one sense we are always traveling, and traveling as if we did not know where we are going; in another sense, we have already arrived.

> We cannot arrive at the perfect possession of God in this
> life, and that is why we are traveling, and in darkness; *but*
> *we already possess Him by grace, and therefore in that sense*
> *we have arrived and are dwelling in the light.*[11]

And so at maximum velocity the train I have been riding bolts
out of its aquatic tube and arches toward the blue sky. For a
moment, everything seems weightless, motionless, as if floating. I resurrect from the watery depths reborn, changed in
the twinkling of an eye, baptized into new life, alive here and
everywhere. As the sunlight streams into the railcar, I wonder if
the prayers of others have helped to pray me where I now am,
somehow born again, momentarily transfigured aboard a railcar
bound for Berkeley.

Entrance to the Downtown Berkeley subway station.

CHRISTOPHER JOHN ROZALES, 2006.

Interior of the Downtown Berkeley subway station.

CHRISTOPHER JOHN ROZALES, 2006.

Stairway to Heaven

Until I began riding the subway to the campus, I never realized how much the Downtown Berkeley station resembles an early Byzantine church or a circular temple. Shafts of light pour through its surrounding windows and bathe the morning commuters in a timeless glow. Those disembarking take a lengthy escalator up through the radiant structure and exit at street level.

As I ascend with fellow riders in a slow, processional manner, I observe how an opposite escalator carries travellers back down into the system. It occurs to me that this illuminated metro station may be imaginatively seen as a heavenly portal leading to and from Paradise. I am reminded of Jacob's famous dream, wherein the Hebrew Patriarch saw angels ascending and descending on a ladder that stretched from heaven to earth (Genesis 28.13).

In a sense, we are like these ministering angels, that is, if we rise out of the subway renewed through in-transit meditation and prayer. The spiritual energy cultivated during a contemplative commute may be extended to everyone throughout the workday, simply by means of a kind greeting, a gentle word.

And on the way back home, after sharing our peace with others, we may once more descend into the railway depths and rejuvenate ourselves through theocentric activity. Via prayerful "metro-meditation," we can rhythmically radiate the light of the heart both under and above ground, if only through the concentrated and sustained power of our thought waves.

In this balanced and communal process, we can work to create a temporary semblance of heaven on earth. We are, after all, mindful beings who possess the inborn capacity to generate (and consciously direct) love. The New Jerusalem itself may be a kingdom where we shall be so filled with Spirit that we cannot help but share it with life beyond the gates. For once we pass on, we may come to enter new worlds in the form of assisting saints, much like in the Buddhist tradition, wherein *Bodhisattvas*, in their sheer love for the whole of creation, ceaselessly help beings enter Nirvana.[12]

As I ride the escalator up through the cascading light beams and glimpse a bit of blue sky overhead, I momentarily imagine myself rising toward heaven, beatifically free to return to the Spirit Mansions of Agape—and go forth again—like the lightning. For Love is not a static thing, but lives, moves, and is perpetually establishing its Being throughout eternity, ever renewing itself for the life of the world. This "mystery of recapitulation" is most palpably felt in living vessels who ardently and joyously seek out the Heart of God, that they might share its infinite, pulsing power with the universe.

Free Man

The trek from the Downtown Berkeley subway station up to the Graduate Theological Union takes about 20 minutes. To get to class, most students cut a path through the campus of the University of California, situated just a few blocks from the metro.

A brisk walk through the university grounds yields an array of idyllic sights—lush lawns and flower gardens, wooden bridges and winding streams, archways, groves of trees, finely wrought gates, neo-classic buildings—all tranquil and inspiring, as a scholastic environment should be. A vibrant, invigorating energy pervades the campus; it pulses with freedom and infinite possibility, the very stuff of youth (and of wise and gifted elder students and professors, some into their 90s, who have grown well, not old).

Exiting at the north gate of the university puts one directly onto Euclid Street, a block-long row of shops and restaurants leading to the GTU. It is here that I would occasionally see a quiet

CHRISTOPHER JOHN ROZALES, 2006.

The campanile and main green at the University of California, Berkeley.

homeless man in red high-top sneakers sitting on the cement near Nefeli's Café. Wiry, long-haired and bearded, he looked about 45. On warm days his shirt would be open, revealing a lean frame similar to the ascetics who live along the Ganges. He usually sat with his arms around his knees, or sometimes with one leg drawn up, arm resting on the knee, a posture that hinted of a relaxed attentiveness. He had a way of looking into people's eyes that did not speak of a man asking for change or a handout (though he gladly accepted money and food when it was given him), but rather one who asked the pointed question, "Who are you? What do you really want?" He looked wiser than his down-and-out condition, and his simple, straightforward bearing seemed to indicate that ultimately, we will take nothing with us except what we have become.

Sometimes I would give him change. At other times I simply tried to acknowledge him with a nod or smile, and he would incline his head or maintain a distant meditative gaze. He was always reserved, silent, except on one occasion, when I happened to see him near Telegraph Avenue, outside the tree-lined Santa Fe Institute of Religion and Art (next to which the homeless receive daily meals). I was going to the Institute to get some books, and out of the blue he came alongside me and asked if I, too, were going to get some food. Whether he remembered me from Euclid Street I don't know, but since I hadn't shaved for a week and was dressed in grungy attire, he apparently took me for a transient.

We exchanged a few words about the heat (it was near summer) and about basic things like having enough water. He told me about a shelter in Berkeley where I could get regular meals and maybe a bed. Then he saw some friends in the gathering crowd and moved over to speak with them.

I remember vividly those few minutes we talked beneath the trees. Our conversation reminded me of my initial days on Patmos, of how when I first came to the isle, I had to scramble to find a cheap place to stay, since the monk who was supposed to take me into the monastery had left for Istanbul. Because of low finances, I lived on canned sardines, bread, and water for a while before entering the monastery.

During those first weeks on Patmos I would attend numerous church services, after which a hearty communal meal was served. Nuns dispensed the food, and they would give me extra loaves of bread to tide me over for a few days. There was something remarkably pure and wholesome about sitting on an old stone dock far from home and eating bread and water, watching the crumbs fall into the sea, and knowing that all my worldly goods, at least for the moment, were in the duffel bag right next to me. There was a kind of serenity, a remarkable lightness of being, a nomadic freedom to be enjoyed. *Via Nuova*, a poem by the modern Greek writer Kostas Ouranis, comes to mind:

> I only want to live now like a rose
> that in mild winter blossoms all alone
> on a low parapet, sunbathed and poor,
> whose whitewashed surface holds the earth in place...[13]

Certainly poverty and homelessness are far from being a romantic adventure. But there is something fundamental (and necessary) about being in constant touch with the basic nature of things, of being in rustic contact with the earth in an organic and unencumbered manner, that cannot be deeply perceived in times of prosperity. One has to live life more on the elemental edge to acutely feel the immediacy and preciousness of the moments given to us through grace. Hence, ascetics advocate that "less is more." And as the Buddhists intone, water can only fill a cup when it is empty.

In June of 2004, as I was leafing through a local newspaper, I spotted a photo of the homeless man in the red high-tops. He had been arrested for public drunkenness and taken to prison. There he had been mistakenly incarcerated with a psychotic inmate who, in a rage, shattered open his skull and savagely beat him to death.

The news shocked me; the violence of his murder was a stark and brutal contrast to the man's gentleness and meditative bearing. But the detail that had the greatest impact on me was his name, which I hadn't known before: Kevin *Freeman*.

A "Free Man"—one who had lived a simple life unfettered by material possessions, and who could, at times, transcend his inner demons and wordlessly impart the importance of living quietly, without attachments—died horribly in the confines of a prison. The story was incredibly and tragically ironic. And yet Kevin is now indeed Free.

Socrates, who also died in a prison, said that we remain incarcerated as long as we live in this fleeting, deteriorating form and existence. He reasoned that death was the ultimate freedom and the most perfect healing, as it jettisons the good from the rigours of a temporal world struggling in ignorance and entropy. For this reason, the Greek philosopher's last words before the hemlock stilled his heart were these: "We owe a sacrifice to the god of medicine." This sacrifice was a rooster, the bird that heralds the dawn and ushers in the beginning of a new Day.

Archway, University of California, Berkeley.

CHRISTOPHER JOHN ROZALES, 2006.

Ockham's Razor

One morning I was sitting in a lecture on medieval philosophy. The professor was droning on and on about "Ockham's Razor." Ockham was a fourteenth-century English logician and Franciscan friar who believed that things unnecessary should be "shaved off" of whatever one is postulating or investigating. Nonessentials should routinely be eliminated in order to maintain clarity.

It was a simple enough concept, yet the professor was making the whole thing extraordinarily complicated, repeatedly bringing up the "Principle of Economy and Parsimony," "Methodological Reductionism and its Phenomenological Implications," how "plurality should not be assumed without necessity...."

Suddenly, a bird landed on the tree branch that just touched the glass of the classroom window and began to sing. This irritated the professor, who walked over toward the window to shoo the bird away.

"Wait, don't do it," I abruptly said to him.

He stopped in front of my desk and arched an eyebrow.

I swallowed a few times and said, "You see, in its stark purity that bird is eliminating anything else there is to say about our subject. The simple, sudden clarity of it sitting on the branch and singing eclipses any need to go on. In some way, Ockham's philosophy—so grounded in simplicity—is all there. Anything else would be too much."

"Are you telling me that a bird has put me out of a job?" replied the professor, feigning sternness.

My classmates and I laughed, and the bird was left to sing.

Ockham's Razor Amplified

I had used the principle of "Ockham's Razor," or a variant of it, on first enrolling in graduate school. Since I had entered a "Theological Union," composed of a wide variety of faiths and traditions, I had to choose a school of affiliation based either on denominational ties or on the study program I wished to pursue. Since there was no Eastern Orthodox School of Theology (or Seminary) and I did not know, on entering, what precise area of theology to study, I was somewhat bewildered. Then I was told by an admissions officer that to make the best possible choice, I would have to examine all the schools—their beliefs, policies, and respective faculty. But there were nine schools and almost as many theological affiliates and centres. Would it be the Jesuits? The Dominicans? The Franciscans? The Unitarian Universalists? I wanted to turn my application in, but could not do so until I chose my school of affiliation.

At this point I remembered the story of the Gordian Knot. Alexander the Great undid a highly complicated knot in the Asian city of Gordium simply by cutting it open with a sword (a move reminiscent of the sharp-edged logic of Ockham). With this in mind, I abruptly left the admissions office and took a brief and to the point campus tour, noticing, with an artistic eye, the architecture of each school's exterior. There were stately Edwardian buildings, Craftsman-type structures, and offices that reminded me of Julia Morgan's style. Of them all, I thought that the brick-lined Dominican School of Philosophy and Theology, situated just opposite the library and located at the top of Holy Hill, was the most classic and imposing, looking like a stately old home from Boston.[14]

In this intuitive, razor-edge manner, I bypassed all scholastic protocol and selected the Dominican School for my general theological studies. Though the move was certainly unorthodox in methodology, it turned out to be the right choice. Among other things, it led me to Mystic Street, the lane that inspired this book and that is located a short distance away from the Dominican Priory and Chapel, where I sometimes attended Mass after class.

CHRISTOPHER JOHN ROZALES, 2006.

The Church Divinity School of the Pacific, formerly the Dominican School of Philosophy and Theology. GTU, Berkeley.

Room with a View

While helping a few classmates settle into their student-housing unit, I noticed that they had made it a point to position their desks alongside windows to take in a view of the skyline. This seemed to be a natural enough choice; as I thought about it, I began to see significant reasons why a room with a view is desirable.

Windows that open to a greater vista give us an enhanced sense of community; though isolated in a dwelling, we still remain connected with the life around us, if only through a view. We can meditate on activity beyond our enclosed state, and may compare or contrast what we see with our own solitary condition. In effect, we are not really alone; our field of focus broadens like a true-to-life movie. The world—with which we share an integral spiritual connection—unfolds before us.

Views have a remarkable ability to rejuvenate the viewer, especially if they open up to land (and sea) scapes. One medical study has demonstrated that patients recover faster after surgery if they are placed in hospital rooms that offer a vista of trees versus the brick wall of an adjoining building. Additionally, these patients took fewer potent analgesics and received less negative evaluative comments in nurses' reports.[15]

Views also instill calmness. Our stress levels diminish as we relax and take in the life around us. Moreover, sight seems to lead naturally into insight. The holy light by which we see, in its infinite range of illumination, ultimately points us to reflect *inwardly*, that we may meditate, pray and come to feel the bright love of heaven emanating in our hearts. Thus the first command voiced by God, an injunction fulminating with both literal and allegorical meaning, "Let there be light!" (Genesis 1.3). Interestingly, St. Augustine, and his mother, St. Monica, while looking out over a flower garden through a balcony window, felt the fire of Agape stirring deep within them; this warmth intensified and "raised their spirits toward the eternal God" *(Confessions* 9.10).[16]

Much like flowers (and all organic life), we are naturally drawn to light. Without light entering our eyes, we cannot see; without light illuminating our surroundings, we inevitably stumble. Our very health, both physically and psychologically, depends on our bodies receiving adequate amounts of sunlight: hence the use of solariums, particularly in hospitals.[17]

Light triggers in us a kind of spiritual photosynthesis—our intellectual (and even intuitive) powers may be said to grow according to the intensity and degree of light to which they are exposed. Perhaps the meditative quality of ancient Greek thought was generated by the unique clarity of Aegean sunlight. And during the Middle Ages, the multi-hued light radiating through the stained glass windows of cathedrals is said to have instilled profound states of metaphysical reverie, catalyzing an internal alchemy of the soul.

Unfolding space, through which light may beam and travel, can also draw us towards an enticing view. Gazing out of a window, we enter into an unbounded dimension far greater than our immediate surroundings and the confines of our finite selves.

When looking out over an expanse, we experience a profound sense of freedom. We are awed by the immensity of it all, and, at the same time, feel intimately at one with it. Something akin to a spiritual passage takes place, hearkening to the holy, infinite avenue by which we came into the world—the "Mystic Street" that leads through this transient realm, and beyond it.

Whether subliminally or overtly, every view reminds us that we are on a never-ending trek through light and space. Every window may therefore be perceived as portal flung wide to eternity.

Music Appreciation

Early in my doctoral program I took a class on the Eastern Orthodox Church. It was taught by a young professor, fresh out of school. Though he was good-natured, his teaching style was not the most captivating, particularly because each session centred on the discussion of chapter readings that were exclusively devoted to the historical aspects of Orthodoxy. Little mention was made of the rich artistic and mystical aspects of the tradition.

A month into the class, a number of the students began wondering when these more expressive, esoteric aspects of Orthodoxy would be aired. One enthusiastic student decided to take matters into her own hands, and in a creative manner. She secreted a CD player beneath the discussion table so that when the professor entered the room, he would hear the mystical, ethereal tones of Eastern Orthodox and Byzantine chanting, exquisite hymns that impel the listener to quietly turn inward and aesthetically experience a semblance of divine rapture.[18] As she exclaimed, it would appear as if the angels themselves were mystically present in chorus! This student had herself been a teacher and knew the value of the arts in reference to learning.

The professor walked in as the music began to play. He took his seat at the head of the table, saying nothing about the chanting, and instead talked about the assigned reading as usual. The woman looked surprised, then glanced at the rest of us. She tapped her ears, indicating that he probably did not hear the music. She cranked up the volume a bit more, yet still the instructor said nothing about it. The class took this as a sign that he was perhaps in a bad mood, and adamantly intent on discussion, so no one said anything about the music. Yet the woman raised the volume even more, and still no reaction from the professor. Eventually, she sheepishly lowered the sound until there was nothing left to be heard. The professor went on with the class, and ended it as he had ended all our previous meetings.

A year later I was descending into the downtown Berkeley subway station to return to San Francisco and heard a terrible scream. When I got to the train platform, I saw the same woman who had played the Byzantine chant selection. She was sitting on a bench, wailing and in tears. The other riders were ignoring her, even though she was sobbing uncontrollably and seemed on the verge of a nervous breakdown.

"What is it?" I asked. "I'm a student at the GTU—we had a class together."

"Oh God, I've wasted a whole year there! I should have been in another program, and now I don't know how I'm going to make up the time!"

"It'll be OK," I assured her. "You'll find a way to make things work."

"No, no, I won't! And it's because no one listens to what I have to say! *No one listens!*"

And with that she stormed into the train that had just arrived and hurtled into the underground darkness. A few months later I learned she had quit her studies altogether.

I do not know what this woman's inner difficulties were, or what problems had driven her out of the doctoral program. What comes to mind when I think of her is her attempt to play music that was never heard.

Z ig and Zag

Between the former Dominican School and the Episcopal School of the GTU is a narrow lane that descends in a long, sharply winding fashion to Ridge Street. While it is a path I would often take to get to the library, sometimes I would resent having to go back and forth to finally arrive at street level. One can clearly see Ridge Street from the path above, so logically the way down should be a simple straight line, but instead, the path inconveniently zigzags, at last ending right at the spot one would have reached with an undeviating linear route.[19]

As my years in graduate school progressed, however, I began to see the wisdom of this road. It is, in effect, symbolic of what goes on in life. Often we see something we desire and wish to have it quickly. The goal is right before our eyes, and we can see a thousand reasons why it should be ours for the taking, yet time and patience are necessary to attain the prize.

This roundabout way of travel teaches us to slow down and appreciate the road we are on, and not just the destination. Indeed, goals and destinations we have planned for ourselves tend to be better appreciated if we struggle a bit and take a little longer to reach them.

Some people get where they have to go quickly and directly—they do not have to travel an arduous distance. But if I were to pause along life's wayside to catch my breath, I would much rather have a conversation with someone like Odysseus, who had a long and meandering journey, than someone who took a bullet train through life. For while all roads lead back Home, to our divine Origin, those souls who took a winding way will most likely have greater stories to share.

Portals of Presence

He was an elderly man with wide, expressive eyes and a neatly trimmed grey beard. One spring morning he held the door open as my classmates and I entered the campus library. Whether he was a professor I couldn't tell, but he seemed to acknowledge each one of us with a welcoming look, the kind given to students on the first day of class.

I was the last to file through. "Come on in, come right on in," he said with a wide grin. The way he said it—so slowly, gently, almost drawling—made me feel relaxed and open, like the door he held. When I turned to thank him, he simply waved his hand with a flourish, hoisted a well-worn book bag over his shoulder, and headed toward the street, a bounce to his step.

I walked into the library and thought of how this man's kind and upbeat spirit had affected me. There was indeed an open-door quality about him—nothing seemed hidden or contrived. He was not performing a good deed while his mind was elsewhere, or simply acting out of courtesy. He was there because he wanted to be, and delighted in helping others. He was a genuine conduit of joy; like him, I also wanted to open doors with a smile and a blessing.

The true mysteries of life accomplish themselves so softly and quietly that they largely go unnoticed, especially because we live in a noisy, hurried world that is mesmerized by spectacle. But then it happens that a stranger gently and happily opens a door, and suddenly revelation is at hand. For a moment everything stops; we smile, sensing that we are right where we should be. We feel something holy and beautiful, and wish to return the feeling. An "energy of openness" irradiates the encounter—all at once we can live without walls. There is no tension left in us. We become transparent, aware at last that only love matters, liberating and uniting Agape, the eternal constant.

The memory of the stranger who so endearingly opened the door stayed with me throughout the morning. I carried his image in my mind; wherever I was going, he was somehow there. And it occurred to me how in this way, good and loving acts go on forever because we take the memory of them everywhere, even into the realm beyond. Thus it may be said that a part of us enters heaven long before we may ever get there; we shall always live in the hearts of those whom we have assisted and loved, and they shall live in us.

Later that day, when I was walking to my car, I saw a father and his young daughter leaving their home. Holding her by the hand, the father stopped by a patch of wildflowers and spoke to her about them, explaining why some petals were orange and others blue. Then he cut a handful of blooms and arranged them in his daughter's hair with such love and devotion that I had to stop and watch for a while. They were both taking simple delight in the joy of the day and in themselves; they were unself-conscious of my presence. I felt their happiness from afar, and was blessed by it.

Love exudes from beings who are deeply interconnected and intensely sharing life; their energy is like the sun, which radiates in all directions equally. Shadows and darkness do not exist in their presence; there is only light, and a kind of timeless quality, effected through the generation of Agape, which is forever.

That night I was going through a book I had come across earlier in the day, the collected writings of Leonardo da Vinci. On the back of a letter dated April, 1476, he wrote, "If there is no love, what then?"[20]

Altar, St. Demetrios Chapel, Patriarch Athenagoras Orthodox Institute, Berkeley.

CHRISTOPHER JOHN ROZALES, 2006.

Moments of Perception

The Patriarch Athenagoras Orthodox Institute at the Graduate
Theological Union is a centre devoted to the study of the
Christian East, promoting the values, teachings, and culture of
Orthodox Christianity. Since a part of my scholastic program
dealt with the study of iconography and the creation of my own
icons, I regularly visited the Institute and made use of its extensive collection of books and materials on the Orthodox tradition.
And when I could, I would attend the Divine Liturgy in the
chapel dedicated to St. Demetrios on the upper floor.

One afternoon I walked over to the Institute to find a book on
Photios Kontoglou (a 20th-century iconographer who favoured
a more rustic, ascetic, back-to-basics method of portraying the
Divine), on whom I was writing a paper. Though I searched the
stacks thoroughly, the volume appeared to be missing. A bit
annoyed, I walked over to a nearby staircase leading up to the
chapel and stood there for a minute, wondering where the book
might be.

Then I heard a voice—feminine, hardly audible, sounding more like a delicate exhalation of breath rather than a voice—say my first name.[21] Had I heard someone speak aloud? I looked around the staircase area; there was no one there.

Baffled, I walked back toward the bookcases and found I was the only person in the stacks. I positioned myself exactly where I heard the voice, to see if I would hear it again. After standing at the spot for a minute or so, I detected nothing at all. However, just within arm's reach lay a few books on a table. Something told me to pick up the nearest one and open it. To my astonishment, I found it to be the very book I had been looking for!

I shivered, thinking about what had happened. How slim were the odds that in the midst of 11,000 volumes I would, by sheer chance, find the book I sought, and in this unprecedented manner! And whose voice did I hear? Memory of the incident returned to me throughout the days that followed. Even now I sometimes wonder about the voice that directed me toward what I was seeking.

And if the voice was an angel's—as some who I have told of the incident have hypothesized—then perhaps the message meant for me was that I should fashion my own "personal icon" (or self-image), just as purely and austerely as Kontoglou had fashioned his art. We are all holy icons in the making, and we paint our image according to how we live and love.

During my initial years of college, an elderly priest I had known came to me in a dream shortly after his death. He said, "When you paint God, use the fullness of your brush." And after my friend Robert Lax passed away, I dreamt that the poet-sage had taken me behind the altar of an old church on Patmos. With a long staff he pointed to the icons, indicating that I should pay heed to their stylistic design and, as well, meditate on the way of the saints.

That morning I drove to school and proceeded to class. A few paces from my car, in the street, lay an artist's paintbrush.

St. Gabriel the Archangel, Holy Trinity Greek Orthodox Church, San Francisco (Robert Andrews, Iconographer).

S.T. GEORGIOU, 2003.

Halos

Throughout my doctoral program I was teaching general Humanities classes at local colleges. When lecturing about the Byzantine civilization, I would organize field trips to the Holy Trinity Greek Orthodox Church in San Francisco, inside of which is a spectacular array of mosaic icons created in the same deeply symbolic and stirring manner as in the days of Byzantium.[22]

During one afternoon visit I noticed that the golden halos of the saints seemed especially bright. As the light filtered through the blue-tinted windows of the church, the radiant disks seemed to incessantly shimmer and swirl in a timeless glow.

The whole notion of halos suddenly intrigued me. Existing both in Western and Eastern religions, they visually define the holy and enlightened. In Orthodoxy, halos demonstrate that those who draw near to Christ increasingly take on his radiance and, by degrees, participate in his glory, a transformative and infinite process termed *theosis*.[23]

Halos encircling the heads (and bodies) of saints also anticipate the time when the whole of creation will be transfigured in God. The sweeping, circular nature of the nimbus microcosmically represents the totality of the reborn cosmos, arranged like a luminous crown. The holy person is therefore depicted as a consecrated caretaker of creation, an anointed steward who helps all things to realize themselves in Christ. The saint becomes a channel or conduit through which the blessings of divine glory may flow.

While meditating on the halos, I noticed that at certain angles they seemed to look green and blue, like the interior of abalone shells or rippling water. This aqueous association triggered my memory, for immediately I recalled a recent visit to a sunny range of coastline located near the church.

A few days before, I had gone there for an early morning run. It was a beautiful summer dawn, and the light was steadily breaking over the cliffs, illuminating the breakers. I had been jogging for nearly an hour and was reaching the far end of the shore, now brilliant in the light of the rising sun. I was quite warm, and waded out into the water to cool off.

Just as I did so, a big crest rolled in and rushed up to my waist, almost knocking me over. A sea of white foam surrounded me, and the reflected light was so boundless and intense, shimmering in all directions, that I nearly had to close my eyes.

For a few ecstatic moments I experienced exceeding brightness and warmth. An otherworldly (and yet organic) purity flooded through my being. I felt as though I were floating into the luminous blue sky, from which I could see a reflection of my image hovering over the waves.

Looking into the halos of the saints at Holy Trinity, I considered that becoming like God (*theosis*) must be something like being encircled by a ring of limitless light, as I had been that morning on the beach. For halos are made of exceeding radiance, as well as an intense and brilliant circumference of heat that does not burn, but rapturously warms and eternally transforms everything into its glory. This is why halos are not merely an age-old means of depicting saints, but are very real, visible, natural outcomes of the deification process—the "Godward journey." Halos are inevitable because those beings who love intensely come to take on the All-Loving Energy that sustains the universe, and they irrepressibly and joyously exude it. Already we are porous creatures through which life breathes and flows; how much more will our transfigured bodies be permeated and suffused with the Light of Eternity! Everything that exists will become open and irradiant, re-baptized in the Agape that shall encircle the whole of paradise, much like a universal halo.

All light and warmth must have a source: in the cosmos, it is the sun; in the body, it is the heart. Yet the ultimate centre of both is God, whom the saints have made their brilliant core and who spontaneously emanate his warmth from deep within themselves, without end. This divine fire is alchemical; it will transform us into co-creators and inheritors of the new world that is to be revealed on the last day.

From the beginning we have been called to love. It is therefore our destiny to become saints—to be holy, to be haloed, if only we let Christ work his Love in us. Through him we were born and reborn and shall yet be born again to become exceeding light within Light. Even now we may walk in brightness as we journey toward the communion of infinite glory.

The Holy Trinity Greek Orthodox Church in San Francisco.

Campus grounds, San Francisco State University, with the Pacific Ocean in the distance.

Walking Through Walls

While the subway train idled in MacArthur Station, the last stop before Berkeley, I watched the sunbeams effortlessly pass through the window of my car. The rays outside had spread within, lighting up the coach. In a similar way, divine Energy gently enters (and dwells inside) everything, perpetually infusing the cosmos. God's glory is instantaneously everywhere; otherwise, nothing could exist.

Then I remembered that the Light of the world, after his resurrection, quietly passed through closed doors and appeared to his disciples at will, almost in the same manner that the Holy Spirit was able to enter the womb of Mary. The metaphysics herein indicates that God imperceptibly transcends his world and is not limited by matter. God can do anything and be anywhere because his infinite Essence precedes and sustains physical life. In him, we too shall one day participate in a supernatural way of being, just as Adam and Eve did before the catastrophic Fall of Creation, undoubtedly the single most divisive tragedy to disaffect life from Life.

As the early Church relates, this initial break with God—caused by human arrogance—rippled like an earthquake throughout the cosmos, for a *sympathia* (a deep and abiding interrelationship) once perfectly united the entire universe. The first couple consequently lost touch with its source of power. No longer could man and woman flow with God as freely as before, going wherever Love would take them, enjoying paradise supernaturally—that is, without being restricted by biophysical laws. Inevitably, the Fall changed the way human beings related to matter and energy: in short, with all of creation.

Einstein discovered in the early 20th century that matter and energy are interchangeable. If this is so, then we could easily pass through walls and alter our molecular structure whenever necessary, just as the resurrected Jesus, the "New Adam," was able to do. But something restricts us from accomplishing this; something altered our freer, dynamic, and more creative interrelationship with energy and matter. This "something" was humankind's break from its original Source. Small wonder that ever since, peoples worldwide have expressed an inborn need for religion, which, in Latin, denotes reconnection. For Christians, this reconnective link is Jesus, the incarnated God-Man who alone could repair the break between Creator and creation. How could any human being right a sin against God and the universe?

In the gospels, Jesus gives us hints of what our reconnected, re-constituted forms will be like, and what powers the resurrected who believe in him will exercise. Like Jesus (and many early saints who, in part, regained their Adamic nature while still in this life), the faithful will be able to pass through matter, radiate a peaceful and joyous luminosity, levitate, even appear in many places simultaneously. These afterlife abilities, which are seen in many religions, would seem almost necessary, considering the manifold needs of love. Perfect love can be exercised only in perfect freedom; hence, there are no limitations for those who wholeheartedly dedicate themselves to Agape.

The resurrected in God shall take on the unrestricted, compassionate qualities of their Creator. They will be gifted with the wings of a new Genesis, that they might fly through the Heart of Eternity, bearing with them the Good News. Yet even now, before the Resurrection, we may share in the joy of the blessed; for, like prayer, when we love intensely, we are everywhere and in everything; we follow the flight path of the Spirit.

An Order of Fish

One mid-morning, after class, I set off to have brunch at a local deli. I hadn't eaten anything since the night before, and for some reason or other, felt like having fish. As I was waiting for my order to arrive, it occurred to me that the first thing Jesus ate, after his resurrection, was a piece of broiled fish (Luke 24.42). I recalled that in early Christianity, Jesus was considered the "Great Fish," as symbolized by the acrostic ICTHYS (meaning Jesus – Christ – God – Son – Saviour). Those fishermen (searchers) who "caught" Christ would mystically consume everlasting Life.

Yet, when the resurrected Jesus eats fish, as Scripture relates, it is something of a reverse process. In this case, emphasis is not on the faithful who partake of their divine Master; rather, it is on Christ Almighty, the God Incarnate who reconsumes what once had supernaturally issued out of him: creation itself. Since the coming of Christ, the cosmos has been increasingly set on a reverse track leading back to its beloved saviour, the supreme embodiment of Agape, that life might be renewed in him.

In eating a piece of fish, the resurrected Jesus figuratively began this inverse process. Moreover, Jesus gave his disciples fish for their breakfast as well (John 21.12), illustrating that those who believe in the Fisher-King will become co-inheritors of a kingdom steadily being renewed in and through Jesus. His infinite love "searches out the depths" (1 Corinthians 2.10) and "draws all 'fishers of the Truth' to himself" (John 12.32).

Artblessings

Shortly after enrolling at the GTU, I happened to walk past the Franciscan School. Through a window I noticed some intriguing paintings. I doubled back and found the office where they were displayed. No one was inside, so I stood by the doorway and studied the colourful, resonant abstracts. I also felt a sense of peace there, for posted on the door was a beautiful welcoming poem.

> May the blessing of light be on you,
> light outside, and light inside.
> May the blessed sunlight shine upon you
> and warm your heart till it glows
> like a great fire, so that the stranger
> may be warmed at it, as well as the friend.
> And may the light shine upon your eyes
> like a candle set in the window,
> bidding the wanderer in out of the storm.[24]

As I finished reading this eloquent greeting, a short-haired, wiry woman in her 50s walked briskly into the office. After introducing herself as the secretary, she asked if I needed any help.

"I just came by to look at the paintings," I said.

"What do you think of them?" she asked.

"I think they're pretty good. They look like a mix of Kandinsky and Jackson Pollock."

"What elect company!" she exclaimed good-naturedly. "I'm the artist."

After brief introductions we began to talk about our mutual interest in art. She then invited me to visit her nearby studio, a tiny room she had termed her "hermitage," in which she spent most of her time when not at work. A happy friendship developed, and for about a year and a half, I would periodically meet her for lunch or a cup of tea. Sometimes we walked out to Shambhala Books on Telegraph Avenue, near U.C. Berkeley, or visited the Nyingma Institute, a Tibetan Buddhist retreat centre. On rainy days, we listened to jazz.

Our conversation topics typically focused on creativity and matters of spirit. And because she learned that I painted, but not with a disciplined regularity, she would chide me for that, as illustrated in a brief quote she had given me by Gertrude Stein.

> And this just about covers everything: The only thing left for a creative artist to do in his life is to do his chosen work in spite of everything and regardless of anything because when living draws to an end, there are no excuses he can make to himself or to anyone else for not having done it.

Either he did it or he did not do it and very often he did
not. Alas, very often he did not.[25]

She thought highly of the psychologist Rollo May and the artist
June Leaf. I learned that she was something of a Jungian and had
a deep interest in hermeticism, alchemy, and spiritual symbolism, which she avidly studied. She saw life as being an endless
series of transformations, and felt that art could be a means of
making these changes happen in a more fluid, positive way.

One evening while we were drinking tea in her living room, we
happened to spot in the fireplace a faint profile of Jesus with a
crown of thorns—the cracks and soot marks had formed the image on brick. This initiated a lengthy conversation about how the
"stone which the builders rejected" (as Jesus refers to himself in
Luke 20.17) may be seen as the Philosopher's Stone of alchemy;
moreover, Christ can be interpreted as the almighty transformative fire through which all things were made, and in whom all
things will be renewed.

Every so often I felt comfortable enough to talk with her about
my personal relationships, which I recall were unsettled at the
time. After a discussion about love and the meaning of marriage,
I remember her writing out for me a pertinent quote by Tolstoy
on the subject. It seemed a bit stern then, but later made greater
sense.

The goal of our life should not be to find joy in marriage,
but to bring more love and truth into the world. We marry
to assist each other in this task. The most selfish and hate-
ful life of all is that of two beings who unite in order to
enjoy life. The highest calling is that of the man who has

dedicated his life to serving God and doing good, and who
unites with a woman in order to further that purpose.[26]

About a year after we met, she asked if I would help her consult
the *I Ching*, an ancient Chinese oracle book. She would not say
why. Through prior conversations she knew that I taught the
world religions, including early divination methods, so with my
assistance she consulted the popular book. Her resultant fortune
indicated that she would be going on a journey.

Some days later she revealed that she had been diagnosed with
breast cancer. Surgery was inevitable, and she wept at the great
change coming in her life.

Months later came worse news. The cancer had spread, and
massive chemotherapy was necessary. Despite her deep beliefs
in the transformative processes of the universe, she was not
comfortable with the thought of dying. "I just want to live and
paint," she would tell me.

Eventually, though, her condition reached the terminal stage.
At her request, she was put on a steady dose of morphine until
she died.

After her funeral, I went by her office in memory, and found it
already reassigned and occupied. But on the door I happened to
find another quote, and as I read it, I felt her speaking the words
to me, for she understood that at heart I was a searcher, as was
she. We had both come to the Graduate Theological Union,
each in our own unique fashion, to find our way in the greater
scheme of things.

> Nothing is more practical than finding God, that is falling
> in love in a quite absolute, final way. What you are in love

with, what seizes your imagination will decide everything. It will decide what will get you out of bed in the morning, what you will do with your evenings, how you will spend your weekends, what you read, what you know, what breaks your heart, and what amazes you with joy and gratitude. Fall in love, stay in love, and it will decide everything.

Pedro Arrupe, S.J.[27]

Crossings

Whenever I brought my lunch to campus, I usually walked over to the Pacific School of Religion and sat on the old steps overlooking Arch Street. This secluded spot offers a stunning view of lower Berkeley and the San Francisco Bay, with the Golden Gate Bridge rising up in the distance. But one afternoon, probably because a dense fog obscured my view, a number of telephone poles popping up from street to street began to occupy my attention. All of them looked like towering crosses from whose wide arms travelled many cables interconnecting the neighbourhood with the world.

In a figurative sense, I considered how the cross of Christ is something of a supercosmic telephone pole linking heaven and earth. Multitudes of prayers, like electronic wires, run to the crucified Saviour who died for the life of the world, and from him reciprocally extend many charged blessings throughout creation.

My spontaneous meditation on the cross of Jesus then deepened. I remembered how an old monk on Patmos repeatedly would say, "I am healed by the cross." But exactly how does the cross heal?

CHRISTOPHER JOHN ROZALES, 2006.

"St. Francis of Assisi with Hands Raised in Blessing," by Benjamin Buffano. San Francisco City College. Arms open wide in blessing, head soaring toward heaven, feet together and rooted in the earth—the human body naturally takes on the shape of a cross.

Certainly the pre-eminent symbol of Christianity denotes love, salvation, resurrection, and protection. The arms of the Cross are open wide; they represent the arms of the Son who welcomes all to himself. He takes on the sufferings of humankind through his own immolation, yet at the same time annihilates all suffering, even death itself, through the power of the resurrection. In essence, love goes beyond the grave, because for the Christian, death is wholly illogical; death is an alien intruder in a world created in loving joy and meant to be happily everlasting. Life was not created to die but to live, and to enjoy the blessings of love forevermore.

And yet to inherit the eternal kingdom, one must crucify oneself, like Jesus, and let go of selfish desires and self-centredness. In this way we become "not self-conscious, but conscious," as Thomas Merton said, and we live in the world interconnectedly. In life's journey we eventually come to see how we are not independent, but *interdependent*. Our shared living stems from a theocentric Source: Christ the Pantocrator, the protective Lord of the Cosmos.

The cross of Jesus also represents balance. Its four equidistant quadrants (as seen in the Greek cross pattern) may be divided into four perfect triangles, which, when multiplied, produce the number twelve, a figure that reminds us of the twelve holy apostles.

Moreover, the cross's horizontal line represents what is *terrestrial* (the earth, the body, the visible and natural), whereas its vertical line delineates that which is *celestial* (the heavenly, the spirit-oriented, the invisible and supernatural). Jesus Christ, being the perfect *Theanthropos*, the God-Man incarnate, is fully represented at the point where the cross intersects, for he is 100 percent human, and 100 percent divine. His Incarnation as God-Man is the necessary means by which humanity may "en-God" itself in the Christ, and so be rescued from a perishing universe bound in entropy. As St. Athanasius proclaimed, "God became man so that man might become God."[28]

In this vein, the cross may also be associated with growth and fruition; it is referred to as a "tree" in the New Testament (Galatians 3.13, 1 Peter 2.24). Indeed, Jesus supplants the "Tree of Life" in Genesis. His life-saving fruit (seen as the Eucharist) is meant to deliver humanity from the wasteland of a fallen world. He is the same Tree who will stand in the paradise of the New Jerusalem and "nourish and heal the nations" (Revelation 22.2).

At this point I rose from the steps where I had been meditating. Slowly stretching, I saw that my own outstretched body—head to the sky, arms open wide, feet together and rooted to the earth—was taking on the shape of a cross!

S.T. GEORGIOU, 1999.

A view of the San Francisco Bay and the Golden Gate Bridge (as seen near the western end of the Graduate Theological Union, Berkeley).

I felt a type of somatic symbolism setting in. My head represented my thoughts, my widespread arms depicted what I held and handled in life, and my legs delineated the path I was on. All four extensions of my "body-cross" led straight to my heart, like the four rivers in Genesis that ran to Eden, indicating that a semblance of Paradise is here and now, within. For good living is about finding one's fertile core, discovering how it relates to the inner and outer life, and then, from the "Nadir of Genesis," radiating out in glory, and sharing the Light with others.

My noontime rumination abruptly ended when the bell tower chimed once, indicating that lunch hour was over. Gathering up my backpack, I headed for class. On my way, a passing seminarian stopped me to ask where Euclid Street was. After giving him directions and exchanging "God bless you"s, it suddenly occurred to me that just then a cross had been formed—two people's life paths had literally crossed, and in a spiritually meaningful way. Each of us would continue to go on our own respective routes, yet that crossing, that "intersection of blessing," would always remain. The energy of the momentary encounter would persist because two conscious, God-powered beings had met and crossed paths peacefully and joyfully, and would, in turn, cross other paths with love.

In essence, a kind of spiritual networking was going on—the net image bringing to mind the great symbolism that the fish (and fishing) played in the teachings of Jesus. For in this life the "great catch" is Agape, and each of us participates in the creation of Love's net through our own everyday crossings. As Jesus intimated, wherever two people meet in the peace and love of God, that place becomes holy, gathered up into heaven.

Upper Cedar Street, Berkeley.

CHRISTOPHER JOHN ROZALES, 2006.

An Ordinary Man

Once a week or so, my father, Ted, accompanied me to campus. He had recently retired, and enjoyed the drive out to sunny Berkeley, sometimes listening to Leonard Cohen tunes en route. After parking in the campus vicinity, we would arrange a departure time for the return trip to San Francisco, then head our separate ways. While I attended class, he would stroll through the neighbourhood and spend the afternoon reading in the library.

One morning we had parked at the top of a long, steep street named Cedar. As usual, we synchronized our watches, then went in opposite directions—he, down Cedar, and I, down Euclid, the cross street. But before I had gone more than a few paces, something called me back to the crest of the intersection. A sudden, deep need ran through me to watch my father walk down the lengthy avenue until I could no longer see him. He became smaller and smaller in the distance, and I thought of how closely the words "father" and "farther" sounded. Father, father... farther, farther...

As he receded from view, I saw his life passing in reverse, as if he were growing younger, steadily becoming a child once more until he finally disappeared. He seemed to be on a road leading back to his beginning, and though I never told him so, that morning I sensed that he would not be with me for much longer.

Less than a year later, close to Easter, this would turn out to be the case. He had a sudden stroke, lost consciousness, and died within a week.

When I walked out of the hospital a few hours after his death, I felt that a chapter of my life had closed. Things would never be the same again. Half of what had created me was gone, and it seemed as though I was striking out on the road very much alone.

Or was I? Could it be that he was still somehow with me, still here in some way, interested in what I was doing, where I was going?

A number of significant things happened just before his death, and soon after it, which gradually gave me the conviction that he was not actually gone, but still walking with me, still somewhere present while I was completing my graduate program. This understanding helped to ease my pain and gave me the inspiration to continue my work.

During my father's last days, I tried to be with him (and with the gathering family) as much as possible. However, at one point, I was torn between staying at his hospital bedside and making a quick trip to the GTU to deliver a highly important presentation that had been scheduled for many months. A priest who came to give a final blessing heard of my dilemma and suggested, in all seriousness, "Let's ask Ted what you should do."

My mother then explained that his stroke had rendered him unconscious. But the priest insisted. So my mother took my father's hand and, in a very concentrated manner, asked him if it would be all right if I gave my talk in Berkeley and quickly returned.

Within seconds his free hand rose from his side, pointed to me, and fell. I took this sudden, incredible gesture to mean that my father was encouraging me to deliver my presentation. Soon after I made it back to the hospital, he died.

The hour of his death was particularly poignant. I was seated just outside his room, reading a book on Robert Lax. In the text was a poem by Henry Vaughn:

> Death is like a Cross, to which many paths lead,
> Some direct, and others winding,
> But ultimately all paths meet in one Center.[29]

Just as I was reading these words, my mother and sister, who were at my father's bedside, called out because he had stopped breathing. On quickly entering the room, I found that he had indeed passed in that moment.

Whenever I was having difficulties with my doctoral program or my dissertation, I would remember the dramatic gesture my father, who had been unconscious for a week, had suddenly made, a sign expressly indicating that he wanted me to finish my work.

How was he able to make that supreme gesture on his deathbed? How could a man who had suffered a severe stroke and who then underwent brain surgery, who continued to bleed in the head and had never regained consciousness, come to some sense of awareness in that moment, and respond so emphatically?

While divine intervention is clearly a factor, I believe that my father was able to do the impossible because he was simply an *ordinary man.* By this I mean that he was God-fearing and God-loving, a family man of few words, honest, rustic, hard-working, straightforward. Ordinary people, when faced with extreme crisis, can accomplish the extraordinary for those they love; they come to recognize and flow with a Power that has all along been working through them, quietly illuminating others.

An ordinary man imparts something more than his temporal, limited self. He does not point to himself, but toward what is infinitely greater. Where many would step forward, an ordinary man takes a step back. An ordinary man would rather listen well than speak. He patiently dims his light so that others may shine. And like the quiet, empty space of a room, so easily dismissed, an ordinary man oftentimes goes unnoticed by a world intent on the spectacular. Yet paradoxically, only those blest to be ordinary become the clear and open channels through which the Almighty Extraordinary can operate and radiate more love and faith into the universe.

Close to a year after my father's death I was going through comprehensive examinations, an extremely gruelling period of doctoral study during which students have been known to drop out of their programs. I had completed my written exams and was about to undergo the three-hour oral, a test that requires an immense amount of preparation. I was walking hastily through the campus to the examination room where my committee was gathering and suddenly thought of my father, wondering where he was in all of this, if perhaps he was looking out for me from his otherworldly vantage point. Just then my foot struck something in the shrubbery, and I saw that I had kicked out of the bushes a pocket-sized copy of the New Testament. At that point I knew that just as my father was in Good Hands, so I would be too.

Angel wrought in stained glass. St. Albert's Dominican Chapel, Oakland, California.

CHRISTOPHER JOHN ROZALES, 2006.

Degrees of Light

I was heading into the subway to catch the Berkeley car when a train roared past. A dust cloud rose from the tracks, its swirling particles illuminated by a bright shaft of sunlight passing through the open canopy above. Had the rays not streamed in at that particular angle, I would not have seen the dust shimmering in the air; it was the degree of light that made all the difference.

The same is true in our regard for the life around us. We note the presence of things not so much because they are there, but because of the degree of illumination accentuating whatever we may encounter. The angular lucidity of our relationship with creation essentially defines everything. The common phrase "Now I see it in a different light" reminds us that while the situation has not changed, our perception of it has.

Likewise, angels are right beside us, but we cannot see or feel them because illuminating grace has not revealed their presence. They are here, perpetually helping creation to sustain itself, yet for the most part we dwell with them unaware of their glory.

But if God were to highlight their incorporeal forms, we would be amazed. Even divine light must shine in a certain way for us to behold what is near, yet invisible.

The right degree of light (heavenly or earthly) can completely change us. When we feel angry, anxious, or depressed, the gentle rays of dawn may help us to forget our problems. The rays shine into us, warming us in a particular way. We move through the sunbeams peacefully illumined, if only for a little while.

When I was on Patmos, I would sit at the pier for hours through the scorching afternoon, barely moving in the harsh, relentless heat. Around 6:30 in the evening, the light became cool and honey-gold, like liquid amber; its colour and intensity shifted, reflecting off the water with such exquisite luminosity that it beckoned to be followed. Robert Lax well understood this "turning of the light"; at this hour he would walk along the shore, oftentimes with friends, and engage in spiritual dialogue. He knew that sky, sun, sea, and earth—all melding in the magic of evening time—could awaken the mind and heart and wholly transfigure the observer. As Henri Bergson said, "Many diverse images, borrowed from different orders of things, may, by convergence of action, direct consciousness to the precise point where there is a certain intuition to be seized."[30]

So much of life passes into us (and us into life) like angles of light—even words. Their vibration and tone, their cadence and rhythm, their meter and pitch may transform us, just as the sunrise can. In truth, we are like living rays shifting and passing into one another, whether by words, deeds, or thoughts.

At certain times our presence alone may illuminate the moment
at hand in unique and penetrating ways. We shine ourselves into
the heart of things, seeking a harmony of convergence, the very
love of God. Even now, our united radiance is forming a brilliant
matrix, much like a kaleidoscopic pattern. Once the design is
complete, there will be a sudden and blinding flashpoint—like
a jet passing over the sun, momentarily obscuring it—and then,
in the new light, we will altogether be changed into something
exceedingly wonderful.

> What no eye has seen,
> what no ear has heard,
> what no heart has ever conceived,
> God has prepared for those who love Him.

1 Corinthians 2.9

Child's Play

While riding the subway to and from Berkeley, I would sometimes observe the behaviour of children in the train. Because
of their natural spontaneity, they were entertaining to watch.
They had nothing to hide, nor were they calculating or cynical. Borrowing a phrase from the Taoist tradition, they were
as "uncarved jade"—bright beings radiating positive, unlimited
potential. Whatever they conceived of did not remain static or
exhaust itself in repetition. Their innocent wonder and lively
curiosity moved from one thing to the next without end. They
were unself-conscious embodiments of the eternal law of nature:
everything is in a ceaseless state of change, and if one is to live
well, it is better to "ride the changes" than become fixed by
them.

A number of things children said and did during my subway
commute have stayed with me. On one trip, a few girls were
incessantly eating black licorice whips. One of them smiled
wide, revealing a row of very white teeth whose vertical spaces
in between were darkly stained, impacted with licorice. When

her friend saw this, she laughingly shouted, "Hey, your tongue looks like it's in jail!" The same pair were later playing with a seashell, putting it to their ears and saying, "I'm calling you on my shell [not 'cell'] phone."

On another occasion, a group of children came on board with their teacher and a few parents. One boy in the group was holding a book upside down by its cover, swaying it back and forth. His friend asked him what he was doing, and the boy happily answered, "Don't the pages look like wings? I'm flapping them—if the book starts to fly, I'll hold on and fly, too!" His comment brought to mind a popular saying by G.K. Chesterton: "Angels can fly because they take themselves lightly."

Another boy in the same group, perhaps five years old, suddenly glimpsed his reflection in the tinted side-window of the car. Instantaneously mesmerized, he started making a host of facial expressions, every so often looking around, as if wondering why no one else had discovered their own reflection.

One child on board appeared to have Down's Syndrome. He seemed expressionless for most of the ride, until a flower seller got on board and handed him a red carnation. The boy accepted it with such awe and reverence, one would have thought he had been given a holy, priceless treasure. He looked at the flower adoringly and repeatedly smiled while cradling it in his hands.

With all these children I felt a close affinity. Their spontaneity and openness, their innocent wonder, joy, and creative sense of play is much needed in a world of cynicism, greed, and exploitation. Jesus understood how babes are naturally suited for the kingdom of God. "Let the children come to me" (Matthew 19.14), he urged his disciples.

Perhaps the very young subliminally remind us that we are all children in God's eyes. Certainly we have the inborn ability to realize our true youthful nature, if only we begin to trust in an infinitely caring Father who loves us more than we love ourselves. It may be that the sole reason why we continue to exist—despite the selfishness and hostility that we may secretly (or ignorantly) harbour within—is that something beyond our reason and understanding simply keeps on loving us.

A Sufi proverb has it that one is born again when the love of God is deeply felt in the heart, even for a moment; if that is the case, then the compassionate will always be forever young.

Here I Am, Lord

On the day of my dissertation proposal defense, where I would seek approval of my intended thesis on Robert Lax, I was understandably nervous. I had been warned by more than one academic that Lax might not be a deep enough subject for a dissertation. His poetry was too minimally oriented to allow for intense metaphysical analysis, they said, and there was little pre-existent scholarship on him; could his life's work be seriously considered for doctoral study? My own graduate committee had similar concerns until I showed them Lax's poems, journals, artwork, and interview material that I had gathered during our visits over the years, and pointed out the existence of the Lax Archives at St. Bonaventure University in New York.

I had spent months preparing the dissertation proposal, and was desperate to begin my work, if only the doctoral council would unanimously give me the green light. My nerves on edge, I decided to walk down the hallway and gaze out of an open window.

While I was catching the incoming breeze, trying to stay calm and cool, I suddenly heard a distant choir. I could not see the singers, but surmised that students were practising their music outdoors. Their voices soothed me, and the song they so movingly sang nearly brought me to tears. Entitled "Here I Am, Lord," the hymn is often sung at funerals, which is where I first heard it: shortly before his death, my father and I attended the memorial service of a professor we both knew, and the hymn was repeatedly sung there.

When I heard the familiar music, I felt as if God was giving me the courage to go forward confidently, as was my father, whom I sensed nearby. The very lyrics suggested that the Lord leads his faithful onward to better things. A great peace then came upon me; I felt ready for whatever would come my way.

Within minutes I was summoned into the Council Chamber. As I was ushered to my chair, I saw written on a corner of the blackboard a single faint word in Greek—an inviting term that happily complemented the hymn I had just heard: *Eltheteh* ("Come forward"). At that moment I knew that my thesis had been cleared for take-off.

Washed Ashore

Throughout my doctoral work, I regularly walked along the beach in San Francisco, from Fort Funston toward Pacifica. It felt good to get out there and forget about everything except the waves, wind, and sky. Academia could get inordinately stuffy, and the ocean offered a satisfying catharsis. As the writer Isak Dinesen expressed, "The cure for anything is salt water: sweat, tears, or the sea."[31]

On weekdays, hardly anyone came to the beach, except for a few fishermen or dog walkers. I might trek for two or three miles down the coast and encounter nothing except a flock of birds, crabs, and an occasional sea lion or porpoise. It was exhilarating to walk the craggy shoreline in perfect space and solitude and feel the pulse of the tides. No wonder so many of Jesus' disciples were fishermen—they rejoiced in the rhythms of nature and life.

The waves incessantly pounded the shore, beating like creation's heart. The sand tingled beneath my feet, as if it were giving me

S.T. GEORGIOU, 2004.

On the beach I had found a large piece of wood shaped like a cross, equidistant on all sides, with a clearly defined circle cut out of its midpoint. It was perched on a high crag of stone, as though raised in worship. *Lower Ocean Beach, near Fort Funston, San Francisco.*

shiatsu massage, which, in effect, it was. The salt air swirled off the sunlit crests, and I drove the free ions deep into my lungs.

At land's end an ecstatic "quickening" came over me, a rapturous metamorphosis effected through nature's primeval rhythms. I felt native in the roaring water and foam, mystically primitive, atavistic.

I had figuratively become like Adam—naked, pure, and open in the world, at one with creation and the elements. In this heightened state, song and verse instantaneously ran through me like mantras:

> They through whom
> the wind flows
> the wind,
> blowing,
> adores;
> they through whom
> the wind flows
> the wind,
> blowing,
> adores...

Sometimes I would pray the age-old Jesus Prayer, one of the earliest invocations of the Church, along the shoreline. Emptying my mind, I repeated (without end), *"Jesus Christ, Son of God, have mercy upon me."*[32]

While in a kind of unself-conscious reverie, I found, over a seven-year span, a wide array of unusual items that had washed ashore in the surf, or were half-hidden in the sand. Often these finds were highly symbolic (or at least I interpreted them to be so). Their unique meanings motivated me to continue studying theology, and to craft theocentric art. I felt that somehow the universe, through grace, was intermittently assisting me in my spiritual journey.

For example, shortly after my father's death, I found his initials, "T.G.," inscribed upon a seaside cliff. A cross was carved between the letters.

And while I had been working on icons of the Virgin Mary, painting her image on driftwood, a board washed ashore with the word *icon* written on it. Later, I found a paintbrush in the dunes.

In the course of a few days I scooped up three clear glass balls, aqua-green and the size of apples, out of the surf. According to Orthodox iconography, a transparent sphere represents the transfigured earth, or the New Jerusalem set apart from the disintegrating realm of matter.

After a storm, I passed below an eroded section of cliff and found protruding out of the sand a waterlogged copy of *Vita Luz* ("Light and Life"), a Christian hymnal.

During one visit I discovered a ladder that had come in with the tide. The waves had flung it in such a manner that it was poised to the sky, intimating the heavenward journey. (In the sixth century, St. John Climachus wrote a famous spiritual text entitled *The Ladder of Divine Ascent*. This ladder was composed of 30 rungs, each step being a virtue to be acquired.[33])

And a few days before Easter, I happened to be walking by the area where I had found my father's initials. As I was thinking of Jesus' resurrection, something glistened in the surf. I reached down into the sand and fished out a small silver cross with a halo radiating from its centre.

While these discoveries were deeply moving, the find that had the greatest metaphysical impact upon me was a large piece of wood shaped like a cross, equidistant on all sides, with a clearly defined circle cut out of its midpoint. It was perched on a high crag of stone, as though raised in worship. I gravitated toward it, and after studying its shape, realized why it attracted me.

This battered, wave-tossed cross from the sea, with its vacant centre and four radiating extensions, perfectly exemplified the mystery of the inexhaustible God who continually empties himself unreservedly to sustain all things. Just as this cross's wide span issued from an empty interior, so God incessantly pours everything out of himself—as illustrated in the sacrifice of Jesus—in order for creation to perpetually exist.

If it were possible to journey into the incomprehensible heart of the Almighty, we would find nothing, for God, being God, needs nothing to exist, yet all things that live are dependent on the unceasing expenditure of his energy. Hence many mystics in both the East and West refer to God as being a continual outpouring "Flow," a fountain-like, incomprehensible Mystery giving of himself without end. This philosophy is evident in the apophatic writings of the Desert Fathers, Rhineland mystics, and St. John of the Cross, and is found in many Buddhist, Hindu, and Kabbalist sources.[34]

Out of perfect love for creation, God "goes out of himself" *(ec-stasis)* and makes himself empty in order that the cosmos might be made complete; his "agapaic emptiness" is, reciprocally, life's fullness. It is upon this emptiness (in essence, *ecstatic Spirit*) that the universe depends; take away the Spirit of Love, and all would vanish. For the driving energy in creation is inexhaustible Agape; in this wholly giving and transfiguring power we are made most real.

In my seaside reveries, I had, in some infinitesimal manner, participated with this power and rejoiced in its dynamic flow. In celebrating the joy of creation, I was, in turn, communing with the joyous Creator. In love I was responding to Love, and consequently discovered spirit-gifts that come to those whose hearts long for God. In a way, whenever I walked along the beach, I too would wash ashore, and rediscover myself in Paradise.

Lower Ocean Beach, San Francisco.

CHRISTOPHER JOHN ROZALES, 2006.

Paying Attention

Once every month or so, on my way back from Berkeley, I would visit my mother at her workplace. She supervised the Community Home-Based Education program for the San Francisco Unified School District. In short, she was a home-school teacher, educating children from kindergarten through the 5th Grade.

Home schooling is just what the name implies: education conducted at home. Children learn in the comfort and safety of their own dwelling, with the help of their parents who follow a carefully prepared lesson plan given to them by the instructor.

The home-schooled pupil usually receives greater focus and care than the student in the regular classroom. Individual needs are directly addressed through weekly meetings with the teacher and lengthy tutorial sessions. Learning is not thought of as a mass-production enterprise where one size fits all, but is structured to suit the specific abilities and talents of the child.

Essentially, the student enrolled in home school is personally mentored by the instructor.

In visiting my mother's classroom over the years, I saw how she instilled in her students what all mentors generate in those they teach: the ability to wake up to the moment—in other words, the power of coming to attention, that lessons might be fluidly grasped.

Attentiveness is indeed indispensable; unless we are attentive, we cannot accurately understand anything in ourselves or others. Take away attentiveness and we would be lost, unable to make keen sense of creation (and the Creator). However, when we simply pay attention to what is around us, psychic doors of communion open—a greater rapport with the universe increasingly develops. We are renewed, and we experience everything with supreme clarity and purity. This tranquility is perhaps best revealed in the face of a child absorbed in thought, or a saint caught up in prayer. Thus Robert Lax wrote:

> Attention is holy;
> that's why
> everyone
> wants it.[35]

My mother's consistent ability to generate attentiveness in her students prompted me to reflect on how this was accomplished. First of all, she was, in herself, a model of attention. She would point out to her pupils how much more they could see, hear, and feel, if only they quieted down and looked around more, listened more. "What shapes did you see in the clouds this morning?" she sometimes asked her students. "And what about those crows—weren't they having a noisy party in the trees? Did you hear them talking to each other, maybe even to us?"

Then I saw how when she directed her undivided attention to a student minding what she was saying, the student, in turn, seemed to slowly awaken. He became increasingly aware of himself and his surroundings, and soon after redirected his newfound attention back to her. It was a reciprocal process, a mutual acknowledgement of being. A kind of opening or channel was created between student and teacher through which both realized that the other deeply mattered, and had unique insights and gifts to share.

It is this sacred communion that, in many ways, constitutes the very basis for learning and is often the underlying reason why students gravitate toward mentors. Someone (other than their own immediate kin) has recognized a spark within, and, in heartfelt love and appreciation of that bright potential, longs to transform the discerned light into an illuminating fire.[36]

As I walked about my mother's classroom, I gradually realized that the student-mentor bond she shared with her pupils did not happen all at once; rather, it was the end product of children stepping into her workspace. Her entire room was carefully designed to foster the three components on which attention (and education) are based: wonder, joy, and love. She knew that students, much like flowers, *gradually* open. Therefore, before pupils would discuss their assignments with her, they would hear relaxing background music; study maps and colourful art displays; read student poetry; handle feathers, shells and other elements of nature; and, if they wished, draw pictures or play musical instruments. As Lax would tell me, "Put yourself in a place where grace can flow."

Looking around the spacious room, I saw many simple yet profound sayings posted on the walls, encouraging and life-affirming injunctions that Lax himself might have composed, such as: "Anything is possible if you believe"; "You are special"; "Be healthy"; "Look more, listen more, love more"; "If it isn't right, don't do it; if it isn't true, don't say it"; "I'm too blessed to be stressed."

Strolling around the brightly lit room, I also saw shimmering mobiles of dinosaurs, butterflies, and fish. One bulletin board featured commonly asked questions, such as "Why is the sky blue?"; "How do plants grow?"; "Where do shooting stars go?" And in case anybody was hungry, there was always a generous basket of food on a counter containing bagels, raisins, and other snacks.

After visiting my mother's classroom, I would adopt similar techniques of fostering attention in my own students at San Francisco State University. Even though I was a college educator, I understood that ambience plays a great part in the learning process, regardless of grade level. Music, illuminating quotes, colourful displays, even the distribution of snacks are excellent and wholesome means by which the mind and heart may more immediately open, and steadily receive enlightenment. Altogether, these techniques help to instill in the student the "mystery of attention," ultimately leading to a direct and edifying encounter between teacher and pupil.

Robert Lax used to tell me that as long as one is attentive, truly present to whatever task is at hand, the time spent in undivided attention will eventually pay off, even though at first this might not seem to be the case. Or, as the philosopher Simone Weil put it,

> If we concentrate our attention on trying to solve, say, a problem of geometry, and if at the end of an hour we are no nearer to doing so than at the beginning, we have nevertheless been making progress each minute of that hour *in another more mysterious dimension*. Without knowing or feeling it, this apparently barren effort has brought more light into the soul....[37]

While I worked on *Mystic Street*, my mother was attentive to my progress. She would regularly ask me how things were coming along with the book. As I was finishing the text, a synchronous encounter took place between us that may confirm how focused awareness indeed pays off, yielding highly unusual (if not mysterious) results.

One evening, my mother brought me a page from her school science manual, thinking I could use it in my writing. The selection explained how white light, through the aid of a prism, may be seen to "magically" contain every colour of the light spectrum. At the very moment she handed me the information, I was typing a sentence on the identical topic: how the supernatural presence of God may seem diffuse at times (like colourless white light), but in reality, the Almighty is perpetually present in manifold and iridescent glory. We need only "prismatic prayer" to demonstrate that God is indeed everywhere, shining out resplendently like all the colours of the rainbow, illuminating those who remain attentive to his love.[38]

CHRISTOPHER JOHN ROZALES, 2006.

The Graduate Theological Union Library, Berkeley. Poised at the top of "Holy Hill," the Flora Lamson Hewlett Library has been acclaimed for its unique architectural design and is one of the most comprehensive theological libraries in the country.

First Impressions

The Flora Lamson Hewlett Library is the nucleus of activity at the Graduate Theological Union. Students of religion and philosophy from throughout the nation make regular use of its extensive collection and archives, and major art exhibits attract many viewers.

Just outside the library is a small courtyard lined with wooden benches. Rows of palm trees sway nearby. With fellow students, I would relax in this quiet, sheltered area between classes.

From time to time, I observed the patrons who came in and out of the library. People-watching is nothing new, but the longer I did it, the more I formed opinions about passersby, momentary estimations based solely on their appearance and body language. I was coming to quick conclusions about people without knowing anything about them.

Judging by appearance can be misleading. It is a bit like flipping through a book and thinking one has read every word—the part is not the whole. Sometimes a man may demonstrate behaviour having nothing at all to do with his basic nature—his actions may simply be the psychic accumulation of whatever he experienced minutes before. Seen in this light, his momentary behaviour cannot be linked with his identity; though he may indeed display a bad mood, it does not necessarily mean that he is at heart a troubled person. Thus our first impressions of people should not necessarily be our lasting ones.

Yet we are prone to form instant opinions—if not resolute judgments—about whomever we may meet, because we have been conditioned to do so. We exist in an impatient, fast-paced, hypercritical society that typically affixes labels on things, not so much to organize, but to more easily define and dismiss. In such a world, no one sees how the seemingly deranged man may be simply crying out for attention, or may even be an angel intent on discovering if people still judge by appearances, as they did with Jesus, who was sometimes dismissed as a lunatic.

All this is not to say that we should refrain from observing one another—it is good to take in the scene. Robert Lax encouraged me to go out into the town and draw sketches of people I thought were interesting, unusual, even provocative. But the moment I started coming to conclusions about my subjects, judging them simply based on their appearance, that's when, said Lax, I should put down my work, dash out into the street with a bowl of soup and give it to someone in need.

Infinite Blessings

One morning, in the college amphitheatre, I was handing out to my students their syllabus. I asked them to come down, row by row, along the side aisles that led to the front of the room, to ensure a more streamlined distribution of the material.

As the one hundred or so pupils filed past, and as I gave them the syllabus in a rhythmic fashion (one to my right, then one to my left), I broke into a smile. Something about their orderly procession and my continual dispensation of the handout gave the whole thing a kind of sacramental air, as if I were a priest bestowing blessed bread to a congregation. Indeed, one student must have perceived this, for when he received the syllabus, he half-bowed and said, "Thank you, Reverend Father!"

Though I laughed aloud at the student's remark, I did, in fact, feel like a minister of some sort. I acutely sensed that I wasn't simply handing out a syllabus, but *blessings*, and these issued not from myself, but emanated from an all-pervasive Power with which everything seemed to flow. Its holy current was sweeping students toward me, and then sending them back out mysteriously empowered, graced with vision and light.

My movements felt not my own. I could see myself happily greeting the pupils, receiving them with joy, handing them their plan of study, yet somehow I stood above and beyond it all, aware only of a greater stream, a Flow that was limitless, coursing through the classroom, swirling through the students and myself, spinning the earth and the sun and every galaxy in heaven.

I could have been standing there for a thousand years going through the same motions, greeting an endless procession of pupils, because the Power moving in all and through all seemed inexhaustible. I was, in effect, passing out parts of a Mystery that was infinite, and in which everything was deeply participating, growing into something incomprehensibly wonderful.

Via infinitesimal degrees, everyone in the room was *becoming*, steadily transforming into the Spirit-Flow circulating through and animating the cosmos. Everything was riding a wavelength of never-ending and increasing holiness, the reality of which lay not in anything fixed, but flowing. And this Flow was without end precisely because the Almighty Source from which it sprang retained nothing for itself, save the spark of life.

As illustrated in the cross with the missing centre that I had found at Ocean Beach, this all-giving Power incessantly empties itself and extends its holy energies everywhere, an act that can be accomplished only by a selfless God who is pure and consummate Love. For as demonstrated in the life, death, and resurrection of his only-begotten Son, *the only power that lasts forever is the energy given away*. True power cannot be hoarded and possessed (this renders the strength of love useless), only ever-extended and shared, and this for the life of the world. Even in the Godhead, in the very heart of the Trinity, we see the Creator in loving communion within his own inviolable and supremely generative Being: the Father ever turns to the Son; the Son ever turns to the Spirit; the Spirit ever turns toward the Father, ad infinitum.

God is a Mystery whose love is freely and unconditionally bestowed upon the world. And yet because nothing in creation can approximate it, his power inevitably returns to its perfect origin, himself, so that it may issue forth again like the beating of an eternal heart. In those fleeting moments when we feel God's cosmic pulse, we perceive infinite and superabundant blessings radiating throughout the universe.

Work of Hidden Hands

At dusk I was walking through the Berkeley hills, idly passing beautiful homes that offered stunning views of the bay. A gentle, golden light filtered through the trees. A relaxed, easy feeling hung in the air.

White picket fences with open gates led into flower gardens. Toys lay strewn over the grass. From big wide oaks dangled old tires transformed into swings. There was this perfect hush, as if the whole world had suddenly retired and decided to pray.

Passing the quiet, illuminated homes, I felt the hands of those who had made them—those who had laid their foundations, hammered in the wood, dug the gardens, planted the seeds. As my fingers ran along the ivy laced fences, I sensed myself touching the work of hidden hands. Something about it seemed sacramental, like receiving a blessing.

On the footpath I walked, with steps cut into it to allow for easier ascent, here, too, I touched the work of hidden hands. A portion of the path was cracked; someone had resurfaced it, whimsically adding bits of mosaic in the cement. Running my fingers over the design, I touched another's touch.

Strolling up the winding lane, it came to me that nearly everything we make contact with has, in some way, passed through the hands of others. Our homes, cars, and computers have, at varying times, been handled. Hands have made our clothes, cooked our food, made up our hotel rooms. We, too, have been created through open hands held and intertwined in love. And all of life is surely the handiwork of God.

In the silent, heartfelt spaces of the day, it is good to feel the many hands that, in love, have held us, and still hold us. We are never really out of touch.

CHRISTOPHER JOHN ROZALES, 2006.

A Date with Spring

A fellow doctoral student once suggested that I meet a friend of hers who happened to teach at San Francisco State University, where for a number of years I had been an instructor. I learned that this woman was a popular professor of drama and, at the same time, exercised a deep and profound spirituality, praying at great lengths daily.

We met at a local coffeehouse near the campus and eventually brought our lattes up to the library courtyard. We had been avidly conversing about spiritual matters, talking about angels in particular, when suddenly she halted in mid-speech, rose from the bench, and quickly walked away. I called out after her but she did not look back. Her inexplicable departure reminded me of George Santayana's abrupt exodus from university teaching. He had been lecturing for a while, and after pausing to look out the window, exited the classroom, saying, "I have a date with spring."

The incident left me troubled. Shortly thereafter, however, things became clearer. I learned through another friend who was in regular touch with the professor that she had been diagnosed with a terminal illness some time before. In such a limbo state, one's actions are not wholly one's own; the dying person is indeed in the greater company of angels. A door begins to open, a portal which only those being called forth can see. Sometimes it opens wider, and those who hear the call, wherever they may be, hasten, and go forward into spring.

CHRISTOPHER JOHN ROZALES, 2006.

Cherry tree in blossom, San Francisco State University.

Gradual Clearing

While lying on the grass in the backyard of the Dominican School, I noticed a thick ring of clouds obscuring the sun. Minutes afterward, the cumulus formations slowly dissipated until the light streamed out of the blue.

The same phenomenon is true when we are listening to someone speak, especially if they have a lot on their mind. At first there may be a dense issue of words, but if we take a step back and listen calmly, the "mists of wordage" blow over, exposing the underlying reason for communication, and the intended message.

People open up to us with all the rhythm, momentum, and intensity of their lives. We may become dizzied by the frenetic energies exerted by those we encounter. That is why, when confronted, it is best to become like a channel through which any overabundance of energy may pass. In letting the "buzz" go by, an articulate listener can focus on the words beneath the words, the unspoken language of the heart. For when people speak, they often hint at what they want to say, and deeper meanings may be audible only in the echoes leading into silence and beyond. Listening to someone is indeed like watching a swirling sky gradually clear.

The German poet Rainer Maria Rilke believed that even spirits of the dead may come to us with all the force and turbulence of their former lives: not to frighten, but in a desperate plea for help. They seek a greater clarity in the world beyond, yet cannot find it, and so they appear before anyone who might listen and offer aid.[39] This would seem to indicate that we should not necessarily be fearful of their strange and ghostly forms, a reflection of their restless state, but instead should pray for their peaceful passage from darkness into light. The effects of prayer, like clouds of incense rising skyward and diffusing into heaven, are subtle and transformative.

Good Shepherd

As I was progressing through graduate studies, I would periodically meet with my parish priest, the late Fr. Anthony, pastor of Holy Trinity Greek Orthodox Church. He would ask how my academic work was coming along and encouraged me to keep up my writing and art. A keen-sighted, tireless man of unwavering faith, he consistently inspired me.

There was a very solid feeling about this priest. When you spoke with him, you knew he was always 100 percent there, and his word was gold. His honesty and straightforwardness were well known throughout the community, and among locals of other faiths and denominations. When he passed away, the street leading to the church had to be closed to make way for the thousands who attended his funeral. At the service, it was remarked that he had once said of his priesthood, "It's as natural to me as breathing."

In his half-century pastorship of Holy Trinity, he never requested a monetary increase, even though he had seven children. He was never seen without his collar and formal priestly attire. With the sole charge of many hundreds of families and acting principal of Holy Trinity Parochial School, he would leave the church late at night and return before sunrise. He never asked for an assistant, and was thus responsible for liturgies, confessions, baptisms, weddings, funerals, hospital visits, Bible study sessions, committee meetings, youth assemblies, and basketball tournaments. Once, when I saw him in the church's exercise centre, I asked him if he ever had time to work out. He smiled and said, "Son, I have heavier weights to lift."

While a man of great intellect, his ways were simple, and his faith, though deeply Trinitarian, did not lend itself to complexity. Every so often he would remind me of Pascal's famous saying: "It is one thing to know God through the head, but quite another thing to love him through the heart."[40] He liked to add that ultimately, God is a "Mystery of Love," and all that God desires is that we respond to his love with compassion, thankfulness, and respect.[41]

In his zeal to minister, he almost seemed to be in two places at once. He could often be found racing from one place to another, and always carried with him the Bible, holy water, and his *epitrachelion* (a long stole worn in administering confession). When his old white Buick roared out of the church parking lot, you knew he was probably off to the hospital to give a final blessing. As he would say, "When God calls, you can't wait."

Once, when he was getting into his car, I mentioned that I was going to see him for confession soon. He asked if something was bothering me, to which I assented. Immediately he got out, put on his *epitrachelion*, and asked me to kneel and confess.

"But we're in the middle of a parking lot!" I protested. "It's a wide open space—there are people around."

He remained immovable. "Confess now. The longer you wait, the harder it will be for you."

So I agreed, and though I felt self-conscious at first, when it was over, I rose to my feet and experienced a profound sense of freedom and inner renewal. It felt good being unburdened beneath the sky.

After his death, many stories began to circulate about his kindness and devotion to the church. Through hundreds of testimonies, it became exceedingly clear that he had given his entire life to God, without reserve or thought to himself. His bearing and ministry exemplified a popular Orthodox maxim by Metropolitan Anthony Bloom of Sourozh: "We should try to live in such a way that if the holy books were lost, they could be rewritten simply by looking at us."

A number of parishioners dreamt of Fr. Anthony on the night of his passing. One of these churchgoers was a young man whom he had visited in the hospital, years before. This youth was then close to death, but after Fr. Anthony lit a vigil lamp and prayed at his bedside, the boy experienced a dramatic change for the better.

In his dream, the young man saw Fr. Anthony clearly. The pastor spoke to him, saying, "A long time ago the Light came for you, but because you were young, and just beginning life, you turned away. Now, at last, the Light has come for me, and I am not turning away; I am going with it."

Seeds of Light

High above the GTU campus in the Berkeley hills lies Tilden Regional Park. One afternoon I went there on a picnic and observed a puppy playing with its owner. So much energy was concentrated in its tiny form; its exuberance seemed perpetual. Children also exhibit this limitless vitality, as do young plants bursting from their seeds. Enormous power has been compressed into the beginning of things, exploding forth like the Big Bang that birthed the cosmos.

When old age comes, energy seems to dissipate. Endurance fails. The body loses its elasticity and curls in upon itself, bowing over.

Yet to the enlightened soul, what is happening is not the end of things, but a recapitulation of their beginning.

Once more we compress into womb-seeds, this time growing in a Body greater than our mother's; we are nourished in the blood and water of the Risen Christ in whom we live, move, and have our being. Via the sheer concentration of Christ's all-embracing love, we freely and exquisitely burst and become like the light of true Light, brilliantly issuing throughout eternity. Our infinitely contracted centre, white-hot in the fireheart of God, breaks open, that new life might flow. We begin again.

Sun of God

During midterm exams, deciding to take a break, I drove out to the beach. It was sunset. The azure sky turned iridescent as the light steadily faded and the sun dipped into the sea.

People had already gathered along the shore. Together we watched nature put on her magnificent show. But why? Was it something other than a stunning visual display? What had called us out to land's end? Why did a holy hush come over us as the sun slipped into the waters, irradiating the horizon with its afterglow? Why did so many linger until darkness came on, and remain staring out to sea?

The setting sun catalyzes metaphysical ideas about death and rebirth. We know that the sun is light and life, yet at day's end it appears to explode and die, leaving a red-gold trail as it sinks beneath the waves. The land quickly becomes cold, like a body bereft of its soul. The star ultimately departs.

Ancients wondered where the sun (or spirit of the sun) travelled after it disappeared from view. Some theorized that it was received by Mother Earth, and was nurtured in her depths until dawn, when she birthed the star anew. Others believed that the orb journeyed into the great beyond, toward a heavenly home, just as liberated souls did. Later, in Alexandrian times, philosophers such as Eratosthenes, who understood that our planet is spherical, theorized that while the sun would set in one region of the globe, it would rise in another. A kind of cosmic continuity came to be associated with the star.

Yet throughout human history, the intense feelings of awe and holiness generated by the setting sun seem to exceed any scientific explanation of the phenomenon. As the fiery orb slips away, an inner longing stirs in us. Perhaps we are drawn toward the sunset because we sense that life is somehow incomplete. We yearn for something greater than our individual and collective

CHRISTOPHER JOHN ROZALES, 2006.

Sunset from Land's End, San Francisco.

selves, for a supernatural reality that exceeds our temporary, dissolutive existence.

The vision of the dying sun accentuates this idea; before us spans a vast horizon, and it swallows the great light of our life. Can this be all there is? Certainly experience tells us that the next day will dawn, and the sun will set once more, but to what end? Why do we feel like something may be missing at dusk? A certain loneliness, even an emptiness, comes on at twilight, like a tired, melancholy man blowing out his bedside candle.

The sunset (and all the longing of the heart associated with it) reminds us that our lives are indeed incomplete and shall be until Christ comes again, the Incarnated Bright Redeemer whom the sun allegorically symbolizes (Psalm 84.11). As St. Paul relates, all of creation is eagerly awaiting this day, when the Almighty King shall return in exceeding glory and restore the universe to its former splendour, as it was in Eden: "The whole creation groans and labours with birth pangs until now, for the cosmos itself will be delivered from corruption into the glorious liberty of the children of God" (Romans 8.21-22).

When the Son at last returns and renews all things in an inconceivably radiant dawn, "The heavens will be glad, the earth will rejoice, the sea will roar, the field will exult, and all the trees and hills of the wood shall sing for joy before the Lord" (Psalms 95.11-13, 98. 7-9). But until the time of "the new heaven and the new earth" (Rev. 21.1), the sun can give us daily hope and promise in the "Light of the world" to come. "Without vision, people perish" (Proverbs 29.18).

Right Time, Right Place

Hasidic Jews believe that people come into our lives for a reason. The well-known Hebrew theologian Martin Buber writes,
"Things seek us out on our paths; whatever comes to meet us
on our way needs us for its way."[42] This "need" often has to do
with a desire for self-empowerment; whether consciously or
subconsciously, people are looking for the inspiration and energy
to continue life's journey. As fellow travellers, we are therefore
meant to strengthen one another in transit, even through the
wave of a hand in greeting, or an emphatic thumbs-up.

There can be deeper, perhaps even salvific reasons why we happen to meet others (and why subsequent friendships develop).
For instance, when we go out with another, we may be escaping
peril that could have arisen during our regular routine. In this
light it is conceivable that an invitation to get together can be
life-saving—in unseen ways, our acquaintances may function as
guardian angels.

While teaching at San Francisco State University, I made friends
with a young woman majoring in art. Over coffee one morning

I asked if I could see her most recent drawings. Since both of us were beachgoers, we decided to meet a few days later at a nearby vista point overlooking the sea, just a five-minute drive from school.

It was about noon when I pulled into the parking lot and drove to a low-lying bluff that led down to the water. She was already there, sitting on a small wooden bench with her sketches. Some were oversized and needed to be spread out, so for more room we sat on the ground.

Suddenly there was a tremendous explosion immediately to our right. The next thing we knew the bench was no more, and a truck was flying in mid-air, heading for the waves. It seemed to hang in the sky for a moment, hurtling in slow motion. Then the roaring vehicle completed its unbelievable arc over the dunes and crashed into the surf, casting water in all directions.

Miraculously, nobody was killed. The driver, who allegedly had his gas pedal lock on him many blocks before, was rescued. The cars and beach walkers he narrowly missed continued on their way. But my friend and I remained in a mild state of shock—had we sat less than ten feet away on the now destroyed bench, we would certainly have been killed.

"I'm glad I met you," she said.

Puzzled, I asked her why that was the first thing she said after the accident.

"You see, nearly every day at noon, I come to this parking lot. Before going down to the beach, I meditate where that bench used to be. I didn't this time because you asked to see my art. If I hadn't met you, I might be dead now."

The New Body

One afternoon in Berkeley, my academic adviser and I were eating at a restaurant on College Avenue, a trendy street lined with coffee houses, bookstores, and a variety of shops. As we watched people go by, we noticed how some strained to glimpse their reflection in the windows of parked cars, at times stopping to give themselves a quick check over. Other passersby paused longer and reapplied makeup or brushed back their hair. And on the walk back to school, I too caught myself momentarily looking at my reflection in the auto glass.

What we had observed over lunch set me thinking about how self-conscious our society is becoming, particularly with regard to appearance. We seem to have a distinct preoccupation with body aesthetics; via the media, we are incessantly urged to refine our looks, even to the point of undergoing "extreme makeovers." How perfect we appear supersedes who we intrinsically are. Mesmerized by the somatic shell, we may neglect to go deeper and honour the spiritual substance.

Such superficiality has its inevitable consequences. The holy essence of our inmost identity ever remains a distant mirage. Instead of looking into our neighbours' eyes with empathy, we may see in them only our skin-deep reflections. Person-to-person communion (and any sense of real community) inevitably erodes. Narcissism (or inferiority-driven isolationism) prevails.

Perhaps the ultimate tragedy is that when we remain self-centred, we can never quite fall in love, for real love centres on self-sacrifice. One who is "in love" is literally *ecstatic*, a Greek word meaning to "go outside oneself." In completely unifying with one's beloved, or with a particular cause or vocation, this abandonment of the self would appear necessary.

And if we cannot love anyone or anything other than ourselves, how can we begin to love God? How can we emerge from our nihilistic isolation and take on a more lasting, integral, communal body—that is, a supernatural form born of Agape—which is the natural course of spiritual evolution? If the seeds of human identity harden, they cannot grow; the seeds of who we are must break open for our interiors to flower throughout creation.

How is this flowering effected? It becomes a matter of redirecting one's inner intent, or, as St. Paul put it, "renewing one's mind" (Romans 12.2). The same energy expended in self-absorption can be reapplied toward developing a greater spiritual body that will never decay and die. While self-centredness leads to an existence disconnected from Creator and creation, a *theocentric* life is infinitely inclusive. Theocentrism holds that since our birth (and rebirth, through baptism), we are meant to experience increasing levels of spiritual awareness that help us grow into the greater Body of God, our fundamental Sourcepoint of Being.

All of creation, "in which God's glory abounds" (Romans 1.20), helps us to do just this. The universe is an organic classroom designed to steer us toward the Creator. Even our natural bodies are made from the same elements that constitute the cosmos, such as oxygen, nitrogen, iron, and carbon. An inborn relationship therefore exists between the human *microcosm* and the universal *macrocosm*. From the Beginning, we were never meant to be isolated, enclosed beings, but were created to cultivate the cosmos and offer it back—many times enhanced—to its Maker. In such an interdependent and nurture-based matrix, nothing can exist alone. Our mere exhalations affect the organic balance of the environment.

When mystics are caught up in divine revelation, they oftentimes see the powerful interrelationship we share with creation, from atoms and cells on up to conscious life forms. They acutely sense the Love of God integrating Matter and Spirit, and intensely feel themselves coursing through their radiant unity. As Thomas Traherne, a seventeenth-century priest and metaphysical poet, wrote,

> You never enjoy the world aright
> Until the sea flows in your veins,
> Until you are clothed with the heavens
> And crowned with the stars...[43]

This revelation clearly demonstrates a going out of oneself and into a greater totality of being. The "old body," so limited and constricted, is no more. Instead, there is a joyous freedom to be found in a universal Body infused with boundless Agape. One feels a communal solidarity born of the Almighty Love "through whom all things were made" (John 1.3), and in whose embracing Image we were created, allowing us to directly interrelate with everything that exists (1 Corinthians 12.12-26).

In letting go of our finite selves, life in the "New Body" is ecstatically experienced as One. The agapaic energy of divine unity transfigures us. A natural and direct kinship is felt with stars, sea-waves, planets, and especially people. All together, life in God is a shared and brilliant journey in intercommunal Love, intensifying as we "become partakers of divine nature" (2 Peter 1.4) and radiate through the Lord's infinite expanse "from glory unto glory" (2 Corinthians 3.18).

Thomas Merton underwent a similar awakening in downtown Louisville. He was walking through the crowded shopping district, when his well-known "revelation of unity" took place. He saw how Love is preeminent because when everything else is abstracted, only Love remains, the bright Joy of God calling all things into life and communion. As Merton ecstatically declared, "All of us are walking around shining like the sun."[44]

"Winged Figure," sculpted by Stephen De Staebler. Graduate Theological Union Library, Berkeley.

CHRISTOPHER JOHN ROZALES, 2006.

Breaking Through

In the centre of the GTU library, illuminated in sunlight, resides *Winged Figure*, a larger-than-life sculpture created by Stephen De Staebler. The soaring bronze masterwork appears to be in transit from this world to the next, as if experiencing divine metamorphosis. Its burnished metal shudders and appears to de-materialize as its spirit breaks free, ecstatically reborn, extending its radiance everywhere.

One morning as I was contemplating the statue, I noticed a woman in front of me whose black hair was naturally highlighted with strands of white. She too was beginning to "break free." The increasing whiteness of her hair revealed that something greater than her mortal form had begun to shine out of her, an irrepressible power that would one day wholly illumine and transfigure her.

As we grow older, the supernatural energy sustaining us starts to break open our temporary bodies. Things fall apart; matter is unable to resist the dawn-rays of the Spirit. Hair turns white, wrinkles appear like cracks creeping across eggshells because something new and everlasting yearns to be born within us. Our hearts long for the Life beyond life, for the realization of the Kingdom of God, and so aging flesh, like an opening chrysalis, gives way—we begin to transform. The very Light of Eternity starts to shine out of us, pulsing stronger than any star, illuminating our heavenward destiny and ultimate apotheosis.

It is interesting to note that when saints are caught up into heaven or experience divine contact, they are usually bathed in white light, the purest emanation of God. Christ himself, when he was transfigured before his apostles, emanated a similar supercharged luminosity: "His garments became intensely white, as no fuller on earth could bleach them" (Mark 9.3).

And so hairs turn white, our wrinkled complexions pale and whiten over time because the holy power that created us and sustained our existence is now stirring in our souls, calling back its own. This irresistible energy, fulminating and supreme, inexhaustibly searches out our depths, that our heart-fire—the bright essence of what we have become—may at last be revealed throughout the universe.

When early Christians passed away, their death was described as *a shining forth*."

Other Power

It happened that a professor teaching one of my classes had to give a paper at a religious studies conference. He appointed a young understudy to substitute for him during his week of absence.

In listening to the lecturer, it steadily became apparent that he had patterned his presentations after his mentor, even down to witticisms and humor. This was not altogether a bad thing, since the professor was an acclaimed speaker, but there was something about the understudy's talks that did not quite work. Aside from an obvious lack of originality, something was missing, or, perhaps more accurately, the lecturer was trying too hard—his forceful attempts in imitating his mentor were getting in the way.

But in the way of exactly what? I thought about how the professor carried himself, how he spoke, and realized that it was not so much the words he said that conveyed power, but the pauses in between. He knew how to articulate the unutterable. He understood how to craft his speech so that when he took a breath, the ensuing silence resonated with meaning. As the Austrian composer Artur Schnabel said, "The spaces in-between the notes—ah, that is where the real art of music resides!"[45]

One can apply this wisdom to everyday life. We may try very hard to make things happen and exert all our might into a particular task, but the final outcome of our efforts does not reside in "self-power" (or *Jariki*, as Shin Buddhists would say), but centres on the mystery of invisible "Other-Power," *Tariki*—on the divine grace and compassion upon which everything depends.

Every so often, it is good to take a step back from whatever we are doing (or feeling) and sense the Spirit of Grace effortlessly flowing from the Creator through creation. Through regular prayer and contemplation, we may learn how to become more sensitive to a Presence greater than ourselves. Increasingly, we become open channels of "Other Power" and better see how love "does not insist on its own way" (1 Corinthians 13.5).

In determining how "Other Power" influences and affects our lives, meditative quiet and patience are required. Hence, in the Hebrew Bible, the Almighty states, "Be still and know that I am God" (Psalm 46.10). Only in the great silence of infinite space, in the "void of unknowing," can we best hear that "still small voice" (1 Kings 19.12), which, in the beginning, whispered, "Let there be light."

Robert Lax used to say, "Try, but be careful you don't try too hard." He understood how our lives should not become so utterly complex that our sense of the Divine Presence gets eclipsed, and hubris results. Rather than self-centredly think, "*My* will be done," we should trust in the gentle words "*Thy* will be done."

This theocentric petition helps us to make daily contact with "Other Power." The words allow us to feel the God of Love praying himself into our hearts, like a king returning home to his kingdom. In turn, we cannot help but respond with spontaneous and genuine love. We open ourselves up and become living conduits of charity and grace, peaceful givers (and receivers) of "Other Power."

Already There

At the West Oakland subway station, the train I was riding came to a stop, as had the car going in the opposite direction. After a minute or so, my train started to move again—or at least I thought it did. What actually happened is that the other train started to accelerate. My car was standing perfectly still, yet the illusion of its movement was profound.

This incident replayed itself in my mind throughout the day. Something about it intrigued me. I thought I was moving—at least for a few moments—but was not. Everything in me believed that I was travelling on to Berkeley, yet I was going nowhere.

At times we journey through life in a similar way. We assume that we are the ones moving as we go about the day, when in reality we are quite stationary. We only think we move because a Power exceedingly greater than our temporary, finite forms is ever in dynamic flow, both in us and around us. Any perceived movement on our part is, in actuality, divine Energy ceaselessly in motion, ecstatically coursing throughout the cosmos.

This Energy—the radiant Love of God—forever seeks itself out in creation, for nothing less than its all-embracing self is more supreme. Divine love can be fully comprehended (and celebrated) only by divine love. In this way, the Eternal Mover brilliantly extends his compassionate light and draws his love-born universe unto himself (John 12.32), while we, in our quiet place of stillness, serve as prayerful channels and witnesses of his glory.

The oft-quoted Biblical phrase "Be still and know that I am God" (Psalm 46.10) simply tells us to become what we already are: reflective vessels filled with the light of God's presence. Both in this life and in the Spirit-filled vastness of eternity, the only thing we can ever truly be is still. We have nowhere to go, because we are already there in God. So, as contemplatives, there is nothing left to do—all doing is effected through the Almighty, who desires that we empty ourselves of our egoistic selves in order to purely *be* in him. So many of life's lessons seem to point to this ultimate teaching.

Sometimes when we pray, God's "doing" and our "being" exquisitely meld, and we encounter the Holy, if only for a while. In these moments of transcendence, we finally come into motion; at last, we are in transit. As the Ojibwa, a North American aboriginal people, like to say, "We feel a Great Wind bearing us across the sky."

Dashboard Madonna

While completing my GTU master's degree, I overheard a professor talking with students who were interested in pursuing a Ph.D. in Theology. "That's something you really have to be certain about," he said rather somberly. "It's an arduous task. There are many ups and downs—the degree takes 100 percent commitment."

At first I was critical of the professor's cautionary tone and lack of encouragement. Later, however, as I moved through my own doctoral program, I saw how there are indeed many ups and downs in earning a Ph.D. The four- to seven-year process may be compared to a mystic's spiritual trek—there are moments of incredible elation, as well as dark nights of the soul during which one may go through excruciating periods of self-doubt, loneliness, and depression.

A general Ph.D. program in Theology consists of three fundamental parts: coursework (including languages and possible fieldwork), comprehensive exams, and the dissertation. The initial period of study tends to be the most interactive, and is, for many, the most memorable. Students come to class and meet with their professors on a regular basis. There is a great variety of lectures and symposia to attend, making this time ripe for social networking.

But as comprehensive exams draw near, students tend to become more withdrawn as they prepare for a rigorous series of tests that examine their areas of specialization. If they pass and become doctoral candidates, they go on to the most solitary stage of the Ph.D. journey: the writing of the dissertation, an original work meant to enhance the discipline or field of study.

Like many doctoral students before me, I had moved through the Ph.D. program at a good pace and had passed my comprehensive exams with distinction. The final and most formidable hurdle was the dissertation. Having had my proposal (on the spiritual elements in Robert Lax's poetry) unanimously approved by the Doctoral Council, what remained was to write the work. This was not as easy as I had first thought.

Though I had carefully assembled my research material and had drafted a detailed outline, I would sit at my desk for hours and essentially produce nothing. I tried writing in different locations and at various times, but the outcome was the same. This went on for many months. Even after numerous consultations with my dissertation adviser, I still could not produce work that withstood scrutiny.

A year passed and I had generated only a half-decent prologue. I locked myself inside for days, swearing I would not emerge until I had written a solid chapter.

But nothing changed. Frustrated, depressed, tormented by collective inertia, I was deep in dissertation hell. I knew exactly what I wanted to write, yet could not express myself. It was as if something was preventing me from doing what I very much wanted to do.

A year and a half into my dilemma I was still "A.B.D."—All But Dissertation. I had tried many means of scholastic salvation, from daily treks to the campus (to get a rhythm flowing) to meditation and exercise. My academic adviser almost washed his hands of me.

And then, one Friday afternoon in May, I was glumly staring out my kitchen window when I happened to see three shabbily dressed adolescents, about high-school age, walk slowly past my car. Their attire seemed to indicate that they were hoodlums, and when one of them loitered by the rear of my vehicle, I was on edge, waiting to see what he might do.

Suddenly he thrust something behind my spare tire, then caught up with his friends. When the trio had rounded the corner, I dashed outside to the car.

At first, I saw nothing. Reaching behind the tire and into the metallic extension supporting it, my fingers closed around what was apparently a thick plastic card. Hastily, I brought it into the light.

I was stunned—the youth who appeared to be a street tough had blessed me with a colourful laminated icon of the Virgin Mary of Medjugorje! Her image was on one side, and a plea to pray to her (and with her) appeared on the other. Ashamed of my earlier suspicions, I read the prayer, and as I did so, felt a prompting to return to my desk and, at long last, begin my dissertation.

Within a week I had written 20 pages. This momentum continued, and I soon realized that whatever had been holding me back from completing my work had been neutralized.

Were the three youths angels in disguise? I may never know, but some time after this incident I received a postcard from a Catholic priest (and friend) in Ireland who told me that he had recently offered Mass for me in Medjugorje. Then another friend gave me a blue rosary that had been passed on to her by someone who had just returned from the holy site. I had no prior contact with Medjugorje, though I had heard of the famous Marian apparitions there.

I still keep the plastic icon-card of Mary in my car. I call her my "Dashboard Madonna."

⌐ull Circle

In the course of finishing the dissertation, I regularly met with my adviser to inform him of my progress. It was always a nice break going over to his house, a beautiful and spacious residence in upper Oakland, nearby Berkeley. The neighbourhood features stately homes with ornate flower gardens. Maple and oak trees line the streets; their intertwined branches meet overhead and form a natural canopy, providing welcome shade in the summer.

Eventually, I finished the final few chapters of my magnum opus and set off to deliver them to my coordinator. As I walked down the lengthy block that leads to his home, I saw in the distance an old man coming toward me. I could tell he was elderly because he was slightly bent over, and was using a sizeable cane. He looked familiar. As he drew nearer, I caught my breath—the figure resembled my mentor Robert Lax, who had died fairly recently. Like Lax, he had a narrow white beard, wore a hat with dangling tassel cords, wielded a cane, and a long shirt hung on his lean frame. Momentarily, I wondered if perhaps I too had passed on, and was now meeting him in the afterlife.

Our paths met. He was an Asian elder; his eyes were opened wide and he was smiling, intimating that he knew me. I looked closer and saw that he was none other than Sifu (Cantonese for "Master"), the past director of the Academy of Chinese Culture in Oakland, a Taoist health institute. Many years before, Sifu had been my first academic employer—I was hired at the Academy to teach a course on the History of Medicine, an area of study that paralleled my interest in the Humanities.

"Good teacher," he said, grinning widely, reaching out to shake my hand. This exclamation was the very same one he would greet me with when I was on his faculty fifteen years before.

After catching up on life, we finally said goodbye and went our separate ways, turning back to wave, happy that we had reunited. But I especially marvelled at the timing of our meeting. Sifu was the first to hire me; now, after handing in the last of my dissertation, I would soon be looking for a tenure-track professorship. When I was working with Sifu as a neophyte lecturer, I was at the very beginning of my scholastic journey; now, on completing my final graduate degree (and having taught at various institutions for many years), I was ending a long period of academic preparation that could lead to a tenured post. Things had come full circle.

Notably, the epilogue of my dissertation, which I also turned in that day, highlighted Robert Lax's interest in the cyclical nature of life. His poetry and drawings indicate that he was fascinated with how the "ends" of things can join with their "beginnings," and so form a flowing unity. He would tell me that this unity is always there, it's just that we have to join end with beginning (or beginning with end) to discover the invisible wholeness of things, just as when a circle is complete when the opposite points of a line at last meet. In other words, we have to keep on living to see how events in our lives are highly cyclical, recurrent, and spiral on to form other unitive connections, from birth to death and life again.

Many world religions believe that the energies of God flow in a cyclical manner, and that it is in our best interest to "go with the flow." As Pythagoras said, "Living well has to do with learning how End links with Beginning." The Bible also demonstrates this chiastic pattern. Everything began in a garden (as illustrated in Genesis 2.8), and everything will end (and start again) in a garden, according to Revelation 2.22.

God seems to like things that revolve (and evolve) circuitously. The cosmos is filled with circular, ovoid, and spinning spiral shapes—atoms, cells, eyes, embryos, the human circulatory system, eggs, seashells, earth, the planets, galaxies, even our very DNA. Altogether, our universe may be likened to a great wheel, a creative round that is turning rhythmically, indeed playfully. And as the Hindu classic the *Bhagavad-Gita* relates, this play, this swirling festive flow is the intercommunal "Dance of Love":

> The Lord resides
> in the heart
> of all creatures,
> making them reel
> magically…[46]

We are like the turning seasons, like the perpetual revolution of night into day, and day into night. We leave our homes in the morning, and then return to them; we left heaven a long time ago, and someday will go back. Our day-to-day living is filled with echoes of this overarching, recurrent reality—in cyclic fashion we return to work, go to the supermarket, attend Mass, visit our family and friends. Our lives are as spirals spirating through eternity, and at certain points of convergence, we meet along the Way.

When Grace Flows

Toward the midpoint of my graduate studies, I wrote a book on the seven-year student–mentor relationship I had experienced with Robert Lax (*The Way of the Dreamcatcher*, 2002). When it was published, a number of serendipitous events and occurrences took place, leading me to wonder if Lax himself wasn't involved in some mystical, playful fashion.

For example, in driving to various readings and book signings, large trucks with "LAX" written across them would glide by and meld into my lane. Of course, "LAX" is a reference to the Los Angeles International Airport, but it was strange how these trucks were appearing more frequently.

When I flew to Louisville, Kentucky, for the 2001 Thomas Merton conference (and to meet with Kevin Burns, my editor, about the basic format of *Dreamcatcher*), I raised my window shade just as the plane came to a stop. Directly below was a cargo container with "LAX" written on it. And a few hours after Kevin and I had decided on the title of the book, we visited Thomas

Merton's hermitage at the Abbey of Gethsemani. On the front porch we were surprised to see a simple wooden bench bearing a brass plate with the words "Bench of Dreams."

As the book received increasing attention, readers (and friends of Lax, mostly from Europe), would forward me their thoughts. Some related how whenever they opened *Dreamcatcher*, they usually turned to a passage that dealt with issues they had on their minds. Others, who kept the book by their bedsides, had peaceful, illuminating dreams, in which Lax sometimes appeared.

In sending their letters, a few readers happened to write a slightly different street address than my own; instead of "Ocean Avenue," they had mistakenly penned "*Olean* Avenue." (Olean was the name of the very small New York town Lax grew up in, near St. Bonaventure University.) And at a GTU trustees party to which I had been invited, I overheard an older trustee discussing Olean. I soon learned that she was the wife of the rabbi who had officiated at the Olean synagogue, which Lax had attended in his formative years (he converted to Catholicism at 28). Thus she knew many of Lax's relatives, including his nieces Marcia Kelly and Connie Brothers. What a small world, I thought! But the Olean connection did not end there. When a *San Francisco Chronicle* reporter came to interview me about the book, it turned out that he was born in Olean.

These strange (though welcome) occurrences also took place on Ocean Beach. During one of my walks along the shore, I met a woman whose father had briefly known Lax—an unusual encounter, to be sure. Shortly after speaking with her, I found a stone with cross-like markings and decided to write the poet's name in the sand with it so that the waves, like undulating prayer flags, would carry his name out to sea. Minutes later, I again looked at the stone and saw that its linear markings on one side also formed "LAX."

Something similar took place at the 2005 Thomas Merton Conference at the University of San Diego, where I gave a paper on Lax, based on my dissertation. After delivering it, I walked outside and found the words "ROB LAX" written into the sidewalk, just behind the main meeting hall. I brought other conference participants to see the writing; they, too, were astonished, especially since the letters had apparently been inscribed in the concrete years ago.

One of the most fascinating coincidences relating to the publication of *Dreamcatcher* transpired at a reading I gave at St. Stephen's Catholic Church in San Francisco. Donald, an Irishman about my age, approached me after the talk. He eventually disclosed that he was the nephew of the late John Main, the famous Benedictine contemplative who had revived the desert fathers' practice of meditation in the West, and around whom the World Community for Christian Meditation had been established.[47] A few days after meeting Donald, as I was reading *When Prophecy Still Had a Voice: The Letters of Thomas Merton and Robert Lax*, I learned that Donald's famous uncle and Lax had met in Canada.[48] Moreover, I discovered that Lax regularly practised the meditation style Main promoted, which emphasizes silent, sustained prayer manifested in the form of peaceful attentiveness. Like Main, Lax believed that clear communication with God does not demand of the seeker a barrage of words, thoughts, or images, but simply a quiet, meditative understanding of God's constant, loving presence.

It occurred to me that many decades before, Main and Lax had shared a mutual appreciation of the contemplative path; now Main's nephew and I were doing the same. Indeed, I would come to visit Donald regularly at St. Dominic's Catholic Church in San Francisco, where he conducts a John Main meditation program.

It is worthwhile to note that shortly after our meeting, Donald asked me to attend a Catholic Mass with him, which I did. Soon after we walked into the church, the Gospel of the day began: "And I, John, was on the isle called Patmos..." (Revelation 1.9). Without realizing it, we went on the feast day of St. John the Divine—the Disciple, Evangelist, and Seer who, according to many early Church fathers, wrote the Gospel of John and Revelation. This was highly significant, since I had met and come to know Robert Lax on the island popularly associated with St. John.

One final "coincidence." I had been invited to speak at another local church. I brought with me a full-length recording of Lax reading various poems, to be played in conjunction with slides depicting his life on Patmos. After the lecture, I was walking with a priest out to my car. All of a sudden we heard Lax's slow, meditative voice saying, "When the wind blows, I listen to the wind; when the rain falls, I listen to the rain...." For a moment we were taken aback, then realized that the tape recorder had inadvertently turned on in my bag. And yet, it was indeed a windy, rainy day...[49]

St. Albert's Dominican Chapel, Oakland.

CHRISTOPHER JOHN ROZALES, 2006.

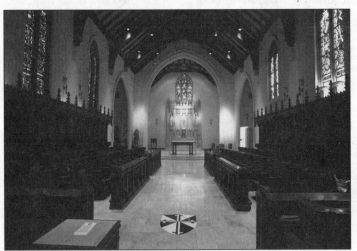

Interior of St. Albert's Dominican Chapel, Oakland.

CHRISTOPHER JOHN ROZALES, 2006.

Timelessness

St. Albert's Dominican Chapel and Priory in Oakland is a spacious complex of Gothic-Tudor buildings surrounded by brick and metal gating. During my first year of graduate work, I did not venture inside, believing the extensive compound to be a private place of worship and study reserved solely for the Dominican brethren.

Then, one evening, I happened to find a central gate open. A handful of people, both men and women, young and old, were filing through, so I followed them.

It must have been winter because the sun was already setting. The fast-falling orb fired the tips of the cypress trees leading to the chapel, making them appear like long rows of burning candles.

When I came to the front door I peered through a grated window and could make out a small congregation inside. I passed through yet another pair of doors and found myself in a warm, welcome space that was dimly lit and intensely quiet.

It was a holy place set apart from the noise and hurry of daily existence. Incense rose from a golden censer hanging by the altar. The last rays of sunset filtered through the stained glass windows and illuminated the white marble floor, highlighting a tiled design of the Dominican cross. The 20 or so people who had gathered stood in prayer or read from their hymnals.

And then Mass began. The solemn, white-robed brothers silently came in and took their places in antique choir stalls that faced one another. One row of brothers raised their voices in song:

> "Glory to the Father,
> and to the Son,
> and to the Holy Spirit."

The opposite row answered, singing:

> "As it was in the beginning,
> is now, and will be forever,
> Amen."

I took a seat close to the entryway and contemplated the harmonic beauty of the chanting and the reverent solidarity of the congregation participating in the hymns. Everything within the chapel encouraged peace, prayer, and rest in God.

As the music echoed and the incense swirled up to the interlacing roof beams, I thought of others who happened to wander into churches during their formative years and were profoundly moved by what they had witnessed. Thomas Merton and Jack Kerouac came to mind. In *The Seven Storey Mountain*, Merton writes:

> I found a place that I hoped would be obscure, over on one side, in the back.... What a revelation it was to discover so

many ordinary people in a place together, more conscious
of God than of one another; not there to show off their
hats, or their clothes, but to pray....[50]

Kerouac, in a letter to Neal Cassidy, reveals his deep love for the
Catholic Church which apparently never left him, despite his
lengthy experimentation with various Eastern faiths:

I cut right along the side aisle till I came to a suitable
solitary spot. Such lovely stillness, such heights of mysterious, upreaching darkness.... I was lost in real sweet
contemplation of what was going on.... I realized that the
church was such a mighty and beautiful thing. It could
stand in Manhattan in 1950 with the same dignity it stood
in Stuttgart in 1450.... That to its lovely meaningful tow-
ers, what did "environment" matter, or history, or what
men had come to or could ever come to? It was a rock of
the ages....[51]

What Merton and Kerouac both discovered was a prayerful
peace and enduring stillness not to be found in a busy, self-
infatuated world. They saw how in church people consciously
(and quietly) return to their divine Source and in loving unison
attain communion with Christ, the Alpha and the Omega.

It came to me then that on entering a church, one is indeed
making direct contact with the Holy. Passage is made into a
supernatural otherworld where the normal sequence of daily
living is suspended in the eternal present of God. This is why
so many have felt a particular timelessness on entering a consecrated sanctuary; they gather in a place specifically dedicated
to the timeless Almighty. Here watches are meaningless, for
"time" implies that things are passing; yet the coming of the

eternal Saviour into the world defies any notion of time. Life is wholly centred in the ever-existent Christ, as the chant I heard on entering the chapel expressed: "As it was in the beginning, is now, and will be forever, Amen."

I looked toward the altar, where a metallic crucifix stood poised between effigies of St. Albert and St. Dominic. Surely the birth of Jesus, his incarnation, crucifixion, and resurrection had super-naturally prepared the universe for its ultimate transfiguration outside of time. His long-awaited coming had altered the normal sequence of life; a new salvific energy had been ushered into the cosmos, and through the holy sacraments and Mass, Christians had been graced with the means to directly access this rejuvenat-ing, transformative Power.

The crucifix I gazed on portrayed Jesus as both sacrifice and ascending saviour. His wide arms were nailed to the cross, and yet simultaneously floated free of it, subtly demonstrating how death (and all the ravages of a fallen world desperately living by the hourglass) had no dominion over him.

In light of this ultimate mystery—the mystery of Christ cruci-fied and resurrected—all things superfluous dissolve. In the silent and eternal presence of the cross (in actuality, a tree of life), only God remains, the sustaining Lord of the Universe. We live solely because his love allows us to, a love that "died for the life of the world" (John 3.16) and resurrected in infinite glory.

Then I saw the priest raise the host. For a moment, he seemed to stretch his arms up like the crucified Son of God, and like Jesus elevating the cup at the Last Supper. At that shared meal, the sacrificial Lamb said, "This is my blood of the New Covenant which is shed for many for the remission of sins" (Matthew 26.28).

Suddenly, the preparation and dispensation of holy communion seemed to me to be the most important thing to do in life. The Eucharist was the great sacrament for which Christ had come, that humankind (and the whole of creation) might be restored. At the heart of the Mass, this restoration is accomplished through the transubstantiation of wheat and wine into the body and blood of Jesus. These organic elements also serve as the spiritual nutrients (or "consecrated culture") from which the "new heaven and new earth" (Revelation 21.1) shall be fashioned. Nothing, therefore, of the original creation will be lost; supreme grace desires that all things be transformed in God, that life may enjoy Life without end.

We, as reverent partakers of the host, are also changed; we "en-God" ourselves in consuming the Eucharist. Once we drink from the holy cup, the timeless God enters into us, and we too become eternal chalices meant to contain and distribute him in love. Our mortality takes on immortality; we realize our role as Spirit-bearers and sharers, created from the beginning to disseminate light and joy forever.

Hummingbird

Early one summer morning, I headed out to the U.C. Berkeley Faculty Club, a renowned redwood structure styled in the Arts and Crafts tradition. A well-known specialist on Buddhist art was going to deliver a lecture there, to be followed by brunch.

The meeting room was on the second floor, adjoining a sundeck. A cool breeze drifted through the open doors. Birds chirped in the nearby trees. There was a laid-back feel to the place, reminiscent of a mountain resort.

Since the staff was still readying the room, I walked out on the deck and breathed in the fresh morning air. As I leaned over the railing and idly took in the campus view, something brushed by my right ear, and then whirred about my head at various points, like a shifting electric fan. Suddenly the source of the sound hovered directly in front of my face, a few inches from my eyes; it was a violet-green hummingbird.

As the Buddhists might say, it was a very Zen moment. In Zen, an Asian meditative practice, one learns how to wake up to the immediate present and feel life instantaneously, in the now.

Indeed, seconds later, after the bird darted away, I reflected on how all my powers of awareness had just peaked; before the hummingbird appeared, I was certainly living, but in my momentary encounter with it, I truly became alive. Through its unexpected visitation, the iridescent creature had directly impressed upon me how everything is here, and now.

I registered no real sense of self in this sudden encounter. There was only a happy sense of hereness, nowness; the intensity of the experience made my perception of the hummingbird wonderfully clear. As Eastern philosophy might relate, "The bird and I became One." There was no need for "self" to comprehend "other"; having momentarily forgotten my self, I was able to see things without preconceptions, without any hint of self-consciousness. Through the hummingbird I glimpsed the cosmos in its original purity, as if for the first time.

But as the seconds passed, and I returned to a more familiar subject-object way of looking at the world, existence became, once again, dichotomous. The immediate sense of unity (not just with the hummingbird, but with everything) was lost. I had returned to looking at creation as Adam and Eve might have experienced it after their expulsion from Eden: suddenly separate from the cosmos they had once been called to nurture.

"Hummingbird moments" or Zen-like encounters happen to us at varying times in our lives. In experiencing them, we briefly feel born again, transfigured, and sense a renewed and enhanced relationship with the universe. When these moments occur, we tap into what may be termed "Genesis consciousness," the pre-Fall psychic state of Adam and Eve, which they enjoyed in Paradise. Since all of humankind is descended from the first couple, it is possible that a remnant of this pure and original superconsciousness exists deep within us, and may be accessed during intense moments of bliss, prayer, and metaphysical enlightenment.

That we tend to forget ourselves (or go out of ourselves) during these deep moments of illumination is intriguing. It seems that in becoming ecstatically and wholly aware of the life around us, personal concerns and self-awareness diminish. There is a suspension of egoistic thought. A kind of inborn selflessness surfaces that detaches the deeply attentive observer from any sense of individual gnosis; only the bliss stimulus (as in the hummingbird) persists which, in turn, catalyzes the realization that love is all, in all.

If it is in my nature to forget myself when engrossed in a love-infused cosmos, a metaphysical question may be raised: What keeps on "remembering me" (when I am no longer consciously aware of myself) that my personal identity may continue? Since deep mystic states cannot be maintained for long in this life, how do I return to a more ordinary sense of self if, for a time, I am entirely absorbed in something (or someone) other than my own being?

It must be that an eternal consciousness (in essence, God) remains present in all human activity, interconnecting every state of psychic and bodily awareness. When we forget ourselves through deep reverie (or through total concern for the other, or via any selfless activity), we eventually come back to a more central, overarching way of living because God "remembers us" while our attention has been ecstatically elsewhere (or momentarily everywhere). God's manifold presence calls us back into the world, that we may once again reintegrate into the basic organic wholeness of the present universe.

It is possible that we sometimes go outside ourselves precisely because subconsciously we sense that ultimate reality is beyond the temporal, ego-oriented "I." Everyone desires something more than what they individually are because deep down we know that our basic identity is in God. As St. Paul says, "It is not I, but Christ in me" (Galatians 2.20). Jesus himself reminds us, "He who desires to save his life will lose it, but whoever loses his life for my sake will find it" (Matthew 16.25). For having found Christ, we will have found Everything.

It may well be that we subliminally seek this Christ when we become deeply absorbed in things outside ourselves, and in others. Perhaps all we are really doing in life is endeavouring to find the Source. Sometimes, though, the Source reaches out through its infinite creation and finds *us*; hummingbirds are always in flight.

Healing Touch

At some point during my doctoral coursework I injured my knee en route to the campus library. Two months after the incident I remarked to a fellow student about how long it was taking to heal. Without hesitation she said, "You really ought to have a priest I know pray over it—he teaches on campus."

Even though I believed in physical restoration through the "laying on of hands" (and had regularly taught a class at San Francisco State University on healing in the ancient world), I had never sought out this form of spiritual therapy. When I began to shy away from the suggestion, indicating that I would wait a little longer for my knee to mend, she insisted that I see the priest at once. So that afternoon, I looked up his office hour, and, on the following day, went to meet him.

It turned out he was a Dominican priest. I had heard of his interest in Christian mysticism and Mariology. But since my visit did not deal with a theological or academic issue, I was somewhat nervous about explaining my reason for dropping in.

I knocked on his door, and when he opened it, I felt a strong sense of joy. The stout, black-bearded father seemed naturally happy, and his bright eyes, accented behind his spectacles, beamed with an almost childish innocence.

"May I help you?" he asked, indicating that I take a seat.

After initial greetings, I felt comfortable enough to tell him that a classmate had pointed me in his direction, and for the express purpose of being healed.

"Certainly we must ask heaven for help," he replied good-naturedly. He was quite relaxed about the whole thing, as if my visit dealt with a familiar scholastic issue rather than prayer therapy. Moreover, he conducted himself with total simplicity and spontaneity; Jesus, Mary, and the saints seemed immediately within reach, because, in truth, they were. The heavenly hierarchy remained ever on call, or at least the straightforward and confident bearing of the jovial priest indicated that a holy energy was readily accessible.

He rolled his chair forward to my side and placed his hands on my knee. Closing his eyes, he addressed his prayer to Christ and the Holy Mother, and very calmly and serenely prayed that my injury be healed.

In a gentle, modulated, reverential voice, he addressed the divine beings as if he were speaking with them face to face. Praying himself into his words, he spoke out of a deep and abiding stillness.

This inner quiet made me still as well—I felt momentarily suspended, floating in some warm and expanding tranquillity. While only the priest and I were in the room, the prayer he softly uttered and the psycho-physical sensations generated from it made me feel like something more was at hand. A definitive silent presence had manifested itself, however briefly, in the course of the prayer. A quiet and luminous fullness had made its healing visitation.

My encounter with the gentle Dominican reminded me of my first meeting with Robert Lax, on the holy isle of Patmos. I experienced a similar feeling of warmth and stillness when I met him, a liberating, restorative peace. And then I remembered the words of Jesus: "Wherever two or more of you are gathered in my name, I am there in the midst of them" (Matthew 18.20).

CHRISTOPHER JOHN ROZALES, 2006.

Holbrook Hall (center) and the Bade Institute of Biblical Archaeology (right). Graduate Theological Union, Berkeley. In addition to its scenic location, the GTU and its environs demonstrate an eclectic range of architectural styles, helping to make study an aesthetic (if not rejuvenating) experience.

Lovechanges

One late afternoon, a classmate and I went for a walk through the Berkeley hills. Throughout our trek we came across a number of elderly couples strolling together, usually with their dogs, although in one amusing instance a man and a woman came around a bend toting their jasmine-wreathed cat in a knapsack.

We remarked that the couples we had encountered seemed to resemble one another faintly, a not uncommon observation; many have perceived that as time passes, people do indeed come to look something like their soulmates (and even like their cherished pets, for that matter).

But how might this phenomenon be explained? It is possible that, over the years, these physical inter-resemblances are psychically effected through concentrated, communal attention and, most especially, fervent love. In essence, we gradually take on the form of whatever we keenly focus on and share life with; eventually, we come to embody and reflect our heart's desire. This deep and sustained devotion is consciously manifested as

Agape, a spiritual love energy which, through its fulminating and constant intensity, may imperceptibly shape matter. It is akin to the fire of divine Love (Isaiah 31.9, John 1.3), through which all things were formed and made.

Whatever lives is changeable, malleable; love particularly changes things and moulds them according to the lover's image of desire. A man so loves a woman that he subtly begins to take on aspects of her features, and a woman so embraces a man, drawing him into the depths of her psyche, that her visage starts to resemble his.

It is interesting how these transformations may be glimpsed in nature, albeit in fainter fashion. A butterfly's recurrent intent to feed on hibiscus leads to its looking very much like the flower; plants, in turning toward the sunlight they need for growth, increasingly become translucent, and take on the brighter colours of the light spectrum. Even lower life forms may thus be said to grow in the direction that love's organic energy takes them; their physical metamorphoses are stimulated by the objects of attraction toward which they gravitate.

While Almighty Love incessantly courses throughout creation, it ultimately completes itself in us, for our higher consciousness helps to link heaven and earth. Only we—the natural-born overseers of life and consummate reflections of the universe—are graced with the overarching ability to channel love back to its holy source.

It would follow, then, that as the cosmos's compassionate stewards, we resemble creation in its entirety more than any other creature. As the Hebrew Kabbalist tradition maintains, our forehead is like the dome of heaven, our two eyes equate with the sun and moon, our lungs exhale like the blowing wind, our stomach is like the churning sea, and our two legs are as the pillars of the earth.

And just as we most completely resemble creation through our ardent affinity with it, so we are also taking on the form of the compassionate Creator, in whose loving image we were fashioned. While we may look increasingly like those we cherish in this life, all lovers of God come to mystically resemble the Lord of Agape via infinitely glorious degrees (2 Corinthians 3.18). Our bodies and spirits are eternally transforming into the exquisite Image of our adoration.

The intimate God in whom we are transmuting, through love, is Christ Almighty—our very own Archetype. Like the wheat and wine of holy communion, we are steadily being transubstantiated into the Saviour's glory. Through the Transfiguration, Jesus himself demonstrated how a body, which intently loves, consequently transforms; according to Scripture, it becomes a beautiful vessel of exceeding light (Matthew 17.2). The more we love God, the more we become light-bearers like him, meant to change others in love, as God has changed (and is changing) the cosmos, preparing it for its ultimate apotheosis.

Z enwhat?

Just over the Golden Gate Bridge and into nearby San Rafael lies Santa Sabina Center, an ecumenical and interfaith retreat facility run by the Dominican Sisters. While in graduate school, I visited there once a month to attend the Thomas Merton Reflection Evenings. On these nights, participants share and discuss select passages from Merton's works, usually in the calm of the Pillow Room, decorated in Asian-Occidental style.

It was Robert Lax who first directed me to this retreat centre. When I met him in 1993, he recommended that I visit Santa Sabina, indicating that it was a scenic and meditative place largely devoted to Merton studies. One evening in late summer I followed his advice, and was overjoyed to find that in addition to books by the famous Trappist, a good number of Lax's own published (and hard to find) works were stocked at the Center.

Over the years, I brought many friends to Santa Sabina. A number were visiting artists from Europe whom I had met on

Patmos and who, like me, would periodically visit Lax to receive creative and spiritual guidance.

Ulf, a painter from Austria, was one such artist. Together we toured the Bay Area for a few days, and the night before he departed for New York, we drove to the wooded compound of Santa Sabina.

After strolling through the surrounding flower gardens, we passed into the ornate cloister and lingered for a while in the chapel, sending out happy prayers to Robert Lax. Then we decided to see if there was anything to eat in the refectory.

En route to the dining hall, we learned that a silent meditation retreat, grounded in the Zen tradition, was taking place on the premises. The participants were, in fact, gathering there for tea and fruit, still maintaining their silence. Though the event was private, neither one of us had eaten all day; quietly we entered the room to gain some sort of sustenance.

Most of the tables were taken, but there was an available one near the entranceway. The table held some fruit and crackers, so we tiptoed in and sat down. Those eating in the silence seemed not to notice us and stared straight ahead, wholly concentrating on each mouthful.

Ulf selected a large, glazed apple, still wet from its recent washing, and picked up a plastic knife to divide and share it. He held it rather firmly with one hand and began cutting into the shiny fruit. The knife was not sharp, so he pressed harder.

Suddenly the apple left his fingers. The force that had been exerted on it sent the fruit flying off the table and skidding down the refectory hall. With a crash it bounced off the distant wall, then shot back till it rolled to a stop at someone's feet.

We looked at each other and tried as hard as we could not to laugh, but the outright humour of the incident was impossible to contain. There we were, gathered in rarefied quiet, surrounded by Zen enthusiasts trying to remain very centred while eating, and out of nowhere an apple had gone noisily flying across the room. The funniest thing was that none of the retreat participants reacted to what had happened—they all continued to calmly eat and meditate!

Doubled over in laughter, Ulf and I hastily exited the refectory and sat on the floor of the hallway, attempting to collect ourselves. For the next few minutes, we kept on referring to the "apple that got away," and burst out in muffled hoots.

But perhaps the most enlightening insight that resulted from all of this happened just as we were about to leave Santa Sabina. A tall, lanky elderly man approached me and said, "I shouldn't be speaking now because I'm part of this retreat. But I just wanted to say that in the dining hall, you fellows were the most Zen of all."

"What do you mean?" I asked.

"Well, when that apple flew off the table, it was probably the funniest thing that happened all evening—it demanded laughter, but nobody laughed except you fellows. Now, I understand we're all trying to meditate here, but from what I know, Zen is about waking up to what's happening right now, in the moment. And what happened back there, well, you boys put the 'zap' into Zen!"

The Still Point

The first time I felt everything come to a virtual standstill was the night I met Robert Lax. As *The Way of the Dreamcatcher* relates, it was a chance meeting. I knew nothing about the man (and next to nothing about his close friend Thomas Merton). After being directed to "the house of the poet," I simply knocked on his door, and after a series of exchanges, was invited into his dimly lit hermitage. He asked me to sit down, and only when he turned fully around and took a seat opposite me did I clearly see his face, a long and narrow visage illuminated by the soft light of a desk lamp.

He looked like a figure in a Rembrandt painting. Though robed in shadows, his ancient, bearded countenance shone out of the darkness. Somehow I felt the warmth of a sunset, the gentle heat of a candle steadily burning, its amber flame motionless, if not mesmerizing.

And yet in no way did he seek to impress (or subliminally influence) me. He was just there, a part of the light, or, better put, a pure and simple channel through which a greater illumination was working.

Indeed, it was almost as if Lax had stepped aside, and something infinitely brighter than both of us was regarding me through his wide, blue-grey eyes. His deep-set, cavernous orbs seemed all-knowing, and, at the same time, all-loving. Everything—the dimly lit room, the surrounding darkness, the wind outside—everything melted away except for his near omniscient (and yet gentle) gaze.

And whatever he could read in me did not seem to affect him, at least not in any outward fashion. He just kept on looking at me, calmly, collectively, trustingly, and I felt like I was being seen for the first time: that is, in the fullness of wisdom and love. Though I sensed that he may have mystically known various things about my past, perhaps even unpleasant things, my faults and trans-gressions seemed not to matter. He simply kept on looking into me, deeper and deeper. His eyes abstracted everything to their immediate essence. Nothing remained except the presence of God uniting us both.

It was as if time and history had shut down. Like a ship poised at the crest of a wave, I found myself hovering, suspended where sea meets sky. What mattered was the fullness of the now-moment, the holiness of the unconditional love that had focused its complete attention on me. Agape had worked its way into my heart; it had opened me, had set about healing whatever secret pain was locked in my depths, had made me aware of Love's timeless and transcendent nature, how it is the only thing that really matters, that truly lasts.

And at some point, I began to respond. I wanted to give back the blessed love that was extending itself my way. I wanted to return the Agape that I was freely being given. As the religious scholar Huston Smith has noted, "Love is an answering phenomenon that melts the barriers of fear, guilt, and self-centredness."[52]

In that brief "still point" I felt everything stop, halted by eyes that could have witnessed all the joy and terror of the world, and yet continued to radiate peace and compassion.

And in that quiet, inviolable space, in the holy intensity of that gaze, I momentarily saw my true self. I was a soul born of divine Love, and would forever be in relationship with that Love. Somehow it all seemed like a dress rehearsal for the last day. In effect, Lax was taking the place of Jesus, asking me (if only through the extraordinary power of his eyes) the ultimate questions that shall rightly centre on the radiant Love that had immolated Itself for the life of the world.

> "Did you love me?"
> "If not me, did you love and nurture my creation?"
> "What did you cherish?"

And then I understood that since everything was created through the Christ ("The light through which all things were made," as John 1.3 intones), I had already been communicating with him from birth, and in a very real, direct way. Christ's immaculate fire radiated on the earth, in the sea, and in the sky, and especially burned in everyone I had ever talked with, walked with, and touched. As Jesus declared, "Whatsoever you do to anyone, you do it also unto Me" (Matthew 25.40).

While I was happy about the good things I had done, I felt a deep remorse about whatever pain I may have brought into the world. I knew that there had been moments in my life when I had wounded not only others—even by a mere thought—but myself as well. And how often had I even forgotten the omnipresence of God, a presence as pervasive and vital as the very breath I incessantly inhaled (and yet could so mindlessly disregard).

All the while, though, Lax's gaze never wavered. His patient, all-embracing eyes kept looking into me, twinkling like stars in their silent and mysterious depths. Something in him knew where my blood ended and my light began. Some infinite part of him (unbeknownst even to himself) understood everything, intimating that everything would be OK.

GIANVITO LO GRECO, 1997.

Robert Lax and the author at the harbour of Skala, Patmos.

$\mathcal{P}$rayer Trails

October–November of 1999 was the last time I journeyed to Greece to meet with the "Poet of Patmos." He died less than a year later, in September, on the Orthodox feast of St. John the Evangelist, the divine Seer and Protector of the Holy Isle.

Lax and I usually met in the evening, which gave me time to read, walk, and meditate during the day. Though summer had passed, the weather was still good, and since the tourist season was over, there was plenty of space to enjoy the isle's rugged, tranquil beauty.

One morning, as I was taking a seaside stroll, I happened to notice a narrow road that led down to a small, crescent-shaped cove shielded by trees. I had never visited this area of shoreline before, and was intrigued. The path wound through an olive grove and brought me to a beautiful and secluded beach, pristine and exquisite. The view out across the sea was clear and limitless, and the quiet was so intense I could hear the trees behind me creak as they swayed in a gentle wind, keeping rhythm with the waves that softly lapped the shore.

What a beautiful and holy place, I thought. And then I saw how others must have thought so as well. Just ahead lay a little whitewashed chapel with a faded blue door and peeling window trim. It was one of those tiny rustic Greek sanctuaries built and maintained by a local family in thanks for divine aid. Usually the door was left unlocked so that passersby might enter and light a votive candle.

I sat in the sand and felt a deep physical-spiritual unity, both in myself and in the environment. Here matter and spirit, the natural and the supernatural, were in blessed balance with one another. A tangible holiness was present, an organic and paradi-

S.T. GEORGIOU, 1999.

Ormos Palou Cove, Patmos.

sical harmony; the shore was like a rich and fertile field, newly tilled, ready to receive seed, water, and light.

And I felt much like a seed. Repeatedly I buried my hands in the moist earth and clenched and unclenched them in the sandy ooze. Shore, sea, and sky seemed to meld and compress in me, as though I were being planted on this rarefied beach. The energies of creation steadily concentrated themselves; their power and beauty were so pure and intense I wanted to cry out and glorify the Creator.

"Praise God, praise God," I whispered. And then I realized that I was spontaneously praying, thanking God for the universe, and for life.

It was a simple prayer, welling up naturally from my heart. The supplication was a eucharistic response to the manifold glory of the cosmos, set into effect by the Almighty. I did not even think the words—they simply came forth by themselves, born of awe and reverence. Over and over I said them; their meter was in sync with the relaxed rhythm of the swaying trees and the incessant, incoming waves. The prayer was my mantra, my spirit-offering, my soul sounding unto God; like the creaking trees and breaking waves, I repeatedly made a natural, concordant sound, a reverberation pleasing to the Lord.

I looked at the wide open sea and said, "Praise God." I looked into the branches behind me, where birds began to sing, and said, "Praise God." I looked into the azure sky flecked with wisps of cloud and said, "Praise God." With each thing I saw and all things I handled I praised the Lord who had made everything possible and real. In deep attentiveness, uniting mind, heart, and soul, I regarded the cosmos as keenly and compassionately as possible, and prayed myself into its life and fruition, saying, again and again, "Praise God."

Then a particular warmth ran through me, and I felt waves of joy and love. I wanted to embrace and be embraced by nature, by everything God had made.

I took off my tank top and sandals and walked down to the surf. The cool water felt exhilarating. Slowly I waded further out, and then plunged in entirely, swimming about 30 metres beyond the shoreline.

Turning around, I saw the mountainous crags of Patmos towering high above me, holy Patmos, with its many churches and shrines, rising up from the sea like a mighty fortress of prayer. For a while I treaded water there and sensed something akin to rebirth; when at last I swam back, it was as if I had stepped on land for the first time.

The salt was thick on my skin and hair; it felt happily coarse, invigorating. I lay on the soft, brilliant beach while the mid-morning sun steadily warmed me. Nothing was on my mind save the clear, effervescent light; I was like a watered plant absorbing it all, tingling, translucent, organically charged. A deep peace flushed through my spirit, and again I said, "Praise God."

After about an hour in the sun, I had a sudden longing to enter the nearby chapel and pray. Certainly I had been praying before, but there was something spiritually enhancing about praying in a place specifically designated and consecrated for communication with God. At that point I wanted to amplify my initial prayers of elation and thanksgiving—I wished to send out intercessory petitions to the whole world. I desired that the entire cosmos be happy, just as I was. It made sense to radiate my spirit-joy to others, to as many as possible.

The old door of the weathered shrine creaked open. Inside was a little space that faintly smelled of charcoal and incense, barely large enough to fit five people. The white stucco walls were unadorned, save for a few icons and two windows on either side. Toward the front, facing the shore, was a tall wooden icon screen portraying Christ, Mother Mary, and the saints, with a small draped altar in the middle. Beyond that I could glimpse the sea and sky through a narrow window.

A few burnt-out, wax-encrusted candles stood in a sandbox near the door, evidence that others had recently offered their petitions. A little lamp burned next to the box, and a glass jar contained fresh candles. I took one and lit it, turning its wick in the fire, and once more said, "Praise God." Then I immersed it in the sand, made the sign of the cross, and moved to the centre of the chapel, standing in silent contemplation.

What to pray for? Family and friends, both living and dead. Anyone I had ever met, or would meet. Prayers:

> For the hundreds of thousands born into the world each day, and the hundreds of thousands passing on. For the sick, the wounded, the suffering, the homeless and abandoned, prisoners and captives everywhere. For the forgiveness and remission of humanity's sins and transgressions, voluntary and involuntary. For all nations and peoples, for their peace and prosperity. For the Holy Churches of God, and for the union of all creation in the Heavenly Father. For the earth, the environment, the myriads of living things, and for the

> stability of the cosmos. For the mercy and protection of
> the Almighty, and for universal salvation. For the triumph
> of peace and love in the world, and for the transfiguration
> of earth into a New Eden.

Except for the sputtering and crackling of the candle, it was very quiet in the chapel. There was a laser-like intensity within, much akin to the exacting focus that takes place in hospital emergency rooms, where physicians deftly attend to the needs of patients.

Indeed, I too was participating in a delicate life-saving operation. Like many others praying for the welfare of the earth, whether in Jerusalem, New York, or Lhasa, my own petitions in Jesus' holy name were medicines meant to help restore a wounded world that in many ways was too distracted, weak, apathetic, or cynical to pray for itself. Certainly I was a part of this "fallen world," but having "put myself in a place where grace could flow" (as Robert Lax was wont to say), I had the holy opportunity to reorient myself and redirect my energies toward communal restoration and salvation. No longer was I living in a noisy, anxious society where the television was always turned on to desperately fill in the blanks, those silent, dark spaces wherein an attentive soul might find God. In the distinct quiet of this blessed shore, I had prayerfully perceived the loving, peaceful Power through which my spirit (and the whole of life) might gently return to the divine Origin of All.

Essentially, I found the beauty of prayer to be threefold: it helps us to communicate with the Creator (and creation); it restores both the supplicant and the cosmos, directing life to its loving Source; and it is the inner interceding means through which the universe may be sustained without end. We may die and leave the earth, but our prayers go on forever, healing and protecting creation unto eternity, for anything good, directed toward God, becomes infinite. Thus the Scriptures repeatedly encourage us to "pray constantly" (1 Thessalonians 5.17), "at all times in the Spirit" (Ephesians 6.18) and "in every place" (1 Timothy 2.8).

A prayer said in complete faith and fullness of heart permeates time and space; it mystically vibrates through every dimension of earth and heaven. It carries with it the irrepressible energy of the Big Bang, and of the Resurrection, even anticipating the Second Coming, because it invokes the ever-present Power through which creation was born, and in which life will one day be transfigured.

Ultimately, prayer is about love. In love, one is moved to pray. If we truly love the universe and the life therein, including ourselves, we will do everything possible to keep the love flowing, that our prayers might have their fullest effect. St. John of Karpathos, a seventh-century monk who lived near Patmos, said, "Above all, don't lose your ability to communicate with God."[53] The channels of communion between our Maker and ourselves must always be kept as clear as possible, precisely tuned to the frequency of love, that we might help to pray everyone (and everything) home.

Footsteps

During one of my research trips to Patmos, I stayed for a few days at a little seaside monastery located in a sheltered, out-of-the-way cove near the main port of Skala. The charming, newly built structure looked like a tiny castle standing on the edge of the shore. It was a small-scale replica of the medieval Monastery of St. John, the island's dominating edifice which served as the primary architectural model for some of the more recent monasteries on Patmos.

On my first day there I attended services in the chapel and performed various monastic duties, such as tending the garden and helping in the kitchen. At some point in the afternoon, I was told by the abbot that the entire community, except for two monks, would be going to the Monastery of St. John for special evening prayers and would return the following morning at sunrise. The remaining two monks and I were then given some final words of instruction.

About 11 p.m., the brothers bade me goodnight and went to their cells. I now had the entire monastery to myself, a rare opportunity. With reverence (and a bit of excitement) I walked around the dimly lit courtyard, then climbed the stone staircase leading to the turreted walls. Moonlight poured onto the sea, and for a while I leaned over a railing and gazed out across the deep.

Around midnight, I descended to my second-storey cell. This comfortable room contained a bed, desk, icon stand, and two windows. One window faced the sea; the other, the shore. Both windows were open wide to the warm summer night air. The near humid heat made sleep difficult, and I lay on my bed hoping the gentle waves lapping the beach would relax me.

Suddenly I heard footsteps in the distance, somewhere along the shore. I listened carefully. They were not scurrying steps, as might befit an animal; they had a human rhythm to them, like a man walking. And yet their cadence was soft, delicate, mysterious—the individual's feet were ever so lightly touching the ground.

With the aid of a flashlight, I looked out of both windows but saw nothing; seconds later, the footsteps ceased. Suspecting the sounds were self-induced, perhaps the product of a momentary dream, I went back to bed.

But they started again. The steps seemed more audible this time, and were right below my shoreline window. Once more I looked out and saw nothing, though all the while the footfalls continued, growing louder. They sounded as if they were winding their way into the lower courtyard; whatever was outside was apparently coming in.

I sat on the edge of my bed wondering what to do. Something was out there, steadily approaching. I was about to bolt out and wake the two monks when suddenly the area around me grew quite hot, warmer than room temperature; moreover, a distinct smell of incense wafted in the air. It lasted only a few seconds, but it was there.

I began to fear. I felt myself caught in the grip of some sort of otherworldly activity. And then, all at once, there was a great crash. It sounded like a heavy table had been pushed down the lengthy outer corridor until it slammed into the wall outside my room.

Immediately I grabbed a thick metal rod (used for propping open a window) and went to the door, waiting for the intruder to force entry. But then I remembered how an hour earlier, when I had retired to my cell, I unconcernedly left my room key dangling from the outside doorknob—after all, I had thought, why worry about security in a monastery? At that moment I decided to take the initiative—I would rush out and confront whoever, whatever was there.

Swinging open the door, I expected the worst, but to my utter astonishment, encountered nothing. I quickly searched the corridor, but found the area to be as quiet and calm as when I had gone to bed.

After a fitful sleep, I awoke at dawn and revealed to the community of monks, now fully assembled, what had taken place. In an almost casual fashion they listened and nodded their heads, as if they had heard it all before. After some deliberation, the general consensus was that I may have been visited by a local saint who had passed away in 1970, a priest-monk of Patmos named Amphilochius Makris, to whom many miracles continue to be ascribed.[54]

When alive, Amphilochius was known for his great powers of clairvoyance, and with them saved numerous people from misfortune and death. He was even known to levitate. A strong proponent of the environment, he planted hundreds of trees on the holy isle and, as well, was instrumental in the construction of various shrines on Patmos, including the monastery I had been visiting. He had also been a friend of Robert Lax.[55]

According to the monks I spoke with—a number of whom had also been visited by this saint—Amphilochius the Elder had come to protect me from an evil presence meant to thwart my spiritual growth. Proof that he had intervened was threefold: the soft advance of his footsteps, the intense heat that I felt in my room, and the pungent (though fleeting) smell of incense. As for the loud crash I heard outside the door, it was the evil that sought to frighten and disorient me, stopped short by the blessed intercession of the saint.

Greek Orthodox tradition maintains that holy men like Amphilochius routinely protect people from harm. As in Roman Catholicism, saintly intercession is an active, not a passive, phenomenon. In fact, there are numerous Orthodox saints interred on various isles of the Mediterranean whose footsteps are sometimes heard by those whom they assist. Among such holy men are St. Spyridon of Corfu (fourth century), St Gerasimos of Cephalonia (sixteenth century), St. Dionysius of Zakynthos (sixteenth century), and St. Nektarios of Aegina (20th century).[56]

Not every monk, however, believed that my paranormal experiences could be so readily linked with Amphilochius the Elder. As one cautious brother told me, it may have been a restless spirit that was responsible for what had happened, perhaps even a poltergeist. Christ himself never denied the existence of ghosts. When he rose from the dead and appeared before his disciples, "they were terrified and frightened, thinking they had seen a spirit" (Luke 24.37). Jesus quelled their fears, saying, "Behold, it is I, myself—handle me and see, for a spirit does not have flesh and bones as you see I have" (Luke 24.39).

Regardless of what I had experienced during those early morning hours, I am ever reminded of the ancient creed of the Christian Church, which distinctly states, "I believe in all things visible and invisible." A well-known quote from Pascal hearkens to this spiritual truth:

> Reason's last step is the recognition that there are an infinite number of things beyond it…. If then natural things are beyond reason, what are we to say about supernatural things?[57]

Whalestone

When the weather was good, I would spend the midterm study period in the tranquillity of Ocean Beach, preparing for exams. On one of these days, I walked down to the shore with my books and spotted a small blackish-grey stone that looked something like a whale. After picking it up, I looked out to sea; to my surprise, a large humpback whale suddenly rose out of the water. Like a missile its huge mass shot up from the depths; it hung over the waves for a moment, then crashed back into the ocean, casting forth a fountain of spray through its blowhole.

The synchronicity of the moment was profound. I clutched the stone tightly, as if through it I could send my surge of awe and exhilaration out to the magnificent creature, swimming less than a mile offshore. The experience left me extraordinarily happy and rejuvenated—I felt an overwhelming affinity for nature, and longed to connect with the wild things of the earth.

This set me thinking about how animals can intensely move us. While observing wildlife or playing with pets, we seem to be changed for the better; somehow we soften and become more tranquil, at ease. It is well documented that numerous psychiatric and emotional ills may be partly remedied through "animal therapy," which is why birds, dogs and other small animals are often found in convalescent homes and correctional facilities.

When whales, porpoises, and sea lions swim along Ocean Beach, an almost reverent hush falls over those watching from the shore. Tensions are alleviated, and a childlike sense of wonder and camaraderie manifests itself among the onlookers. People relax and feel a warm and vibrant connection with each other and with all of life. They sense the restoration of a "missing wholeness," the loving unity of Eden.

In making a heartfelt connection with creatures, perhaps we are recalling the original duty of humanity: to care for creation, and through love and compassion tend the garden that is earth. Certainly this was Adam and Eve's great role, which all of us have inherited. From the beginning we have been called to exercise a fellowship with every living thing. To have "dominion over life" (Ecclesiastes 16.24) does not mean to dominate creation, but to preserve nature and cultivate the cosmos in love. Thus the first man and woman named the creatures and saw how each has its own distinct temperament and characteristics, its individual and irreplaceable ethos. Everything that comes into life is therefore holy and blessed, praising its Maker uniquely, simply by existing.

It is this inter-organic and cosmic holiness that we long for when we feel a closeness with animals. We are subtly reminded of how deep our interrelationship with them was before the Fall took place, before an inherited brokenness—stemming from Adam and Eve's disobedience—disaffected us from the Creator and from creation itself.

When the first couple rebelled (through an arrogant pride that set in motion the greed, violence, and wastefulness of humanity), the entire universe suffered, including the animal kingdom. Thus wild things are skittish around us; they avoid contact, for they have little, if any, memory of the original peace shared in Eden. They have forgotten who we are, just as we may have forgotten how they were created to be our beloved companions, helping us, in their own blessed way, to praise God and to pray for the good of creation.

Only the saints, it seems, have managed to restore the loving bond that had existed between human beings and animals. Through their intense compassion, these holy men and women have regained the pre-Fall blessedness of Adam and Eve, allowing them to communicate freely with creation. They flow with the love that created the cosmos, the integrative energy that living things best respond to. As stories of the saints tell us, creatures become tame in their hallowed presence, and even the barren wilderness issues and blooms in abundance.[58]

In our current age of great environmental callousness and blatant disregard for the fragility of the animal species, we may still see evidence of the original bond of love and fellowship that we once shared with creatures. In December of 2005, a 50-foot humpback whale was entangled in heavily weighted crab lines near the Farallon Islands, about eighteen miles west of San Francisco.[59] It was struggling mightily, endeavouring to keep its blowhole out of the water. A rescue effort was immediately co-ordinated; a team of divers swam around the whale, attempting to cut it free from the many ropes that had ensnared it. This was an extremely risky manoeuvre, since the mere flip of a humpback's massive tail can kill a human.

According to the divers, the whale became quiet, floating in an almost passive fashion throughout its rescue, giving off a steady rhythmic vibration. When at last it realized that it was free, it began swimming in circles around its liberators. Then, in an apparent display of thankful affection, the whale carefully approached each of the divers and gently nuzzled them. After floating for a while in their midst, continually emitting vibrations, it left for the open sea.[60]

Isaac of Nineveh, a seventh-century desert saint, writes movingly of love's role in uniting creation and drawing us closer to the animal world. His words demonstrate that the heart of one who loves everything beats to sustain not only the individual self, but especially the life of the cosmos.

> And what is a loving heart? It is the heart's burning for all of creation, for men, for birds, for animals.... At the remembrance and at the sight of them, the merciful man's eyes fill with tears which arise from the great compassion that urges his heart. It grows tender and cannot endure hearing or seeing any injury or slight sorrow to anything in creation. Because of this, such a man continually offers tearful prayers, that all things may be guarded and forgiven.[61]

Priest of Dreams

After Robert Lax's death in 2000, he appeared to me in numerous dreams. Because Lax was fond of dreams and believed that they were a means by which heaven communicated with earth (and the primary medium through which the dead could make contact with the living[62]), I paid particular attention to the dreams I had of him, and recorded them carefully. Usually they took place in his hermitage on Patmos, although every so often we would encounter each other along the seaside pier where we used to walk, in an old countryside church, or on Ocean Beach in San Francisco.

The demeanour of the poet-sage was usually bright. His wide, ancient eyes were almost always smiling, encouraging. At times he was deeply meditative, but he ended up laughing heartily, just as he did when he was alive.

The first dream I had of Lax occurred a few months after his death. He was about to move to a new home and was giving away his possessions. He turned to me and asked, "What do you want?" Rather boldly, I replied, "Your house." He smiled and said, "You know you can't have that." Then I asked him, "What can I have?" And he bent down and kissed the small gold cross around my neck. In essence, Lax had demonstrated that the greatest gift was already within my possession: the presence and love of the Almighty—the "treasure within which does not grow old or fail" (Luke 12:33). It is this interior treasure that lies hidden in our souls, awaiting discovery. Thus Thomas Merton wrote, "Our real journey in life is interior; it is a matter of growth, deepening, and of an ever greater surrender to the creative love and grace in our hearts."[63]

A number of the dreams I had of Lax dealt with transit—a natural enough theme, since he was making a transition from this world to the next. In a few of them I saw his house carried up into the air, as if by a tornado, like Dorothy's house before it landed in Oz.

In one of these dreams I was inside the hermitage, conversing with the poet. We both knew the house was being carried away, but were unconcerned. We went on talking as in the days when I would visit Lax on late summer evenings and the wind would be blowing hard outside, creating high-pitched whistling sounds that we would listen to at length and comment on. Even though the dream indicated that Lax was departing this life (evidenced by his airborne hermitage), it also gave me the feeling that somehow I would always be travelling with him; our connection would remain intact. As he had told me the last time I had visited him, "We'll always be strolling up and down that old harbour [on Patmos]."[64]

Other dreams had more to do with my academic and artistic progress. In these, Lax and I usually walked along the shore, and he would give me intermittent words of counsel. What words we exchanged didn't always come through, but it was enough to have seen him in my sleep, knowing that he was, in some way, with me. On these walks he would share various writings or point out the iconwork in a seaside chapel and encourage me to keep up my own creative pursuits.

In one dream we had returned to his hermitage. He opened a large, elegantly bound book filled with unintelligible script, arcane writing that looked like Chinese characters. Each letter was a complex (though aesthetically rendered) labyrinth of lines and squiggles. He kept on looking at me and laughing, nodding his head as if I knew (or would one day know) what the writing meant. Perhaps in some way the characters represented my journey in life—perhaps having crossed to the other side, Lax had some kind of access to the "Book of Life."

A few dreams centred on my dissertation (which largely focused on the spiritual elements in Lax's poetry). Because my concurrent teaching had, for a while, addled the rhythm of my writing, I was trying very hard to finish the academic work on time. At one point, when I was under much pressure, I dreamt that I was jogging along Ocean Beach. It was a foggy day. While running through the mist, I saw in the distance a man who looked like Lax. Increasing my speed, I came closer, and saw that it was indeed him. Then I began to note that the closer I raced to my mentor, the faster I found myself running. And when I finally reached him, I was sprinting at such a phenomenal rate of speed that I could not stop. He disappeared behind me, sadly waving goodbye.

I woke up with a start and realized that the dream was about slowing down my academic pace. As Lax had repeatedly told me when he was alive, the best work is accomplished when one is calm and relaxed, quietly gathered in a tranquil inner state. Thinking, writing, learning (and living) become so much easier then. Rather than graduate that semester, I finished my doctoral program the following year, and was all the better for it.

Lax sometimes admonished me in my dreams. In one, as I was walking with him along the Patmos waterfront, I asked, "Don't you think there are too many spiritual books out there? There's something of a glut, isn't there?" To which he sternly replied, "No, they'll never be enough! One book, one word can reach someone at the right time and make all the difference in the world!" Then he suddenly narrowed his eyes and asked, "Why do you still follow me around, anyway?"

Perhaps my most memorable dream of Lax took place close to the time of his death. It was set in a small whitewashed church containing various mosaics of saints, akin to those in Ravenna. Gathered in the front pews were many young people Lax had counselled and inspired over the years, mostly writers, artists, and intrepid searchers from Europe and the States. I found myself among them, sitting with the poet Gary Bauer, the singer and dancer Galatea Psonis, the painters Niko Eliou, Ulf Knaus, Markus Rotzer, Gianvito Lo Greco, and Olivier de Kerchove. Everyone was looking toward the altar with an air of increasing expectancy.

Then Lax emerged from the right side. He was dressed in the all-white outfit he used to wear periodically on Patmos, a long jacket with baggy pants, but somehow in the church it looked like a robe—indeed, like a priestly vestment. His hands were raised and his face was very bright, full of wonder. He approached the front of the simple stone altar and looked upward, toward the apse, as if communing with God. He stood there motionless for a while, then turned to us and smiled.

Slowly, with movements that hinted of ritual, he descended the altar stairway and walked over to where we sat. With each carefully measured step he seemed increasingly to radiate. Then he asked us to come closer, and when we rose and gathered round him, he whispered with awe and deep affection, "They let me say Mass! They let me say Mass!"

With a beautiful smile, brimming with infinite love, he regarded us for a final time, turned around, and, as if leading an invisible procession, went up the steps to the altar. Everything then disappeared in a blaze of light.

Body Wisdom

As I was hurrying to class one evening, it struck me that I was going in a forward direction—I was made and meant to *go forward*. As obvious as this would seem, it had never really dawned on me that we are beings created to consistently move in this way. We stride onward, step after step. We gain ground and forge ahead. Ours is a progressive passage—we were born to advance.

While briskly walking, I noticed how as one of my feet went down, the other slightly lifted into the air. In a sense, I was attached to the earth, and yet a part of me momentarily strove to break free from earthly confines. Suddenly I felt myself to be *independent* (liberated of physical restrictions, as demonstrated by one foot rising), and, at the same time, *dependent* (one foot ever remains on earth, indicating that our material forms are bound to the organic matter from which they came). Walking consequently demonstrates that a part of us longs to ascend and take otherworldly flight, while another part is comfortably in touch with the earth. Our steps lead us to discover how this life is about finding a balance between the heavenly and the earthly, the supernatural and the natural, the spirit and the body. It is the beginning of a long journey leading to cosmic equilibrium in Christ, the transfigured God-Man in whom the physical and spiritual are harmonically unified.

Our bodies, in so many ways, can teach us valuable metaphysical lessons. Study of our anatomy and physiology can lead to illuminating spiritual insights. For instance, in briefly scanning our frontal exteriors (without using a mirror), we can see nearly all of them except for our own faces, our own heads.

Can there be a higher meaning in this? Since we cannot see our own heads, perhaps this indicates that we become "somatically complete" by acknowledging (and communicating with) the heads of those around us. In this light, the heads of other people make our own bodies whole; likewise, those who seek to connect with us do so via eye and facial (i.e. head) contact. We are, in essence, interacting parts of each other—together we make up a greater body.

When two people closely face each other, their profiles form an intriguing holistic pattern. Not only do they form a chalice (seen in the shared space between their faces), but the space separating their entire frontal bodies takes on the appearance of a vessel. Consequently, when two people meet, the potential for a subtle kind of communion exists; a type of interpersonal eucharist can take place, an exchange of love and spiritual gifts.

The form our bodies take on their very own is fascinating. While we can simulate a wide range of shapes in nature, overall, we seem to most look like trees. Our legs are like trunks, our toes like roots, our arms, fingers, and heads like branches extending toward the sky. At the same time, if we spread wide our arms and legs, we resemble five-pointed stars. And whether as trees or stars, we seem to be constructed to extend and grow, to radiate outward, like seeds bursting from the soil and starlight firing its way through the depths of space. Our basic shape indicates that we are made to reach out and make contact with all of life. Even the human interior demonstrates this; our arteries, nervous system, and neuron pathways "branch out" like trees and swirl like microcosmic galaxies.

In examining our exterior covering, we appear to take on the texture of earth's natural terrain. The skin of our backs is like the smooth and barren desert, whereas that on our scalps may be likened to tangled forest growth. If we closely inspect our finger and toe prints, we see swirling patterns in our skin—wave-like, cloud-like—suggesting that we are clothed in the organic dress of sea and sky.

And just as the environment features rolling hills, valleys, fissures, and caves, so we also have a similar somatic landscape. We too undulate and dip, have crevices and recesses. Moreover, like the earth, our bodies are largely composed of water, and our streams go deep underground. And just like the earth, our spirit-centre (the heart) is like a fiery core. The microcosmic body is therefore a reflection of the macrocosmic earth, as so many ancients understood.

Scanning our exteriors, we find in our midsections the umbilicus, the link through which we were once bodily connected to our mothers (and, in a metaphysical sense, to all human life that came before us, leading to the first couple in Eden). Small wonder that this access point is precisely located in the midsection of the body, as it was once our central lifeline to existence. Chinese and Indian physiology has it that in this axial area the vital energy of the universe *(Chi/Prana)* is most deeply concentrated, and can be thought of as a great heat, an inner fire. In Christian terms this analogy is understandable, considering how the birth cord simulates humanity's greater link to God, the "holy and consuming Fire" from which we came (Hebrews 12.29) and in which we shall be transfigured.

That the umbilicus is centrally located in the body serves as a continual reminder of the Almighty Fire that gave us life, the sole energy through which we continue to exist. Meditating on our navels can thus visually and symbolically inspire us to live theocentrically—to recollect God the Fire-Source.

As with our navels, our sex organs are located in the midsection area, and are also powerful sources of heat; moreover, they have the particular capacity to generate life. They microcosmically simulate the agapaic Fire that created the universe, hence their central placement in the soma. Seen in this light, sex is, in its purest form, a holy act born of love, vital to the stability and survival of humanity and the cosmos as we know it.

The only part of our bodies uncovered by skin are our eyes, the "lamps of the body" (Matthew 6.22). Because they are exposed and have depth, ancients termed them "the windows of the soul." In their scintillating vastness, the spirit-core of a person was thought to be visible.

Irises can also resemble swirling galaxies, newborn stars exploding into form. So when we peer into another's eyes, we might imagine that we are glimpsing the brilliant birth of the universe.

In this way, seeing (made possible through the "Light of the World"), becomes a perpetually renewing and illuminating experience, especially as it is accomplished through the bright Power that "makes all things new" (Revelation 21.5).

Body language, especially that of hands, also bestows a type of spiritual wisdom; it reveals inner intent. If someone gives something to another with both hands, a more intimate sense of giving is imparted; if done casually, with one hand, the gesture seems less meaningful.

Closed hands oftentimes display hostility or fear; nothing except tension and violence can be exercised with them. Open, fluid hands are far more useful, both to oneself and to one's community. Through them, love can be palpably given and received in countless ways.

The most common bodily gestures are circular. We often make rotary movements with our hands and arms, and we are always turning and twisting our heads and bodies. These motions seemingly trace the circular patterns and ovoid forms seen in much of life, from eyes to embryos to the earth itself. Perhaps this is so because with circles, every ending is, in essence, a new beginning, an eternal round of rebirth.

Above all, the human blood flow continually courses through the body in a circulatory manner; like the sun and the moon it takes an orbicular path. The process begins in the heart and returns to it. As winter becomes spring, so the blood flows in a perpetual cycle. What issues forth comes back around to its origin.

The same may be said for our souls. Our spirits have left home (that is, God), and yet they travel in the body of creation, ever anticipating and moving forward toward the day when they shall return to their divine Origin. To a degree, they are already there, because the Creator is ever with us, as we are in Him. As St. Catherine of Siena said, "All the way (back) to heaven is heaven."

Infinite metaphysical meanings can be gleaned through the study of human anatomy and physiology. Created in the "divine Image," we reflect aspects of the All within all. Thus in the *City of God*, St. Augustine, the fifth-century Church father, was led to write:

> Quite apart from practical purposes, there is in a man's body such a rhythm, poise, symmetry, and beauty that it is hard to decide whether it was the uses or the higher beauty of the body that the Creator had most in mind…What I am thinking of is the rhythm of relationships, the *harmonia*, as the Greeks would say, whereby the whole body, inside and out, can be looked upon as a kind of organ with a music all its own. The beauty of this music no one has yet discovered because no one has dared look for it. Nevertheless, if this total organic and cosmic design could only be discerned, even in the seemingly ugly elements of the human viscera, there would be revealed to the soul so ravishing a beauty that no visible shapeliness of form that delights the eye could be compared with it.[65]

Cleaning Chalkboards

Since I was a GTU graduate student during the day, most of the college classes I taught in San Francisco were scheduled in the evening; they ended rather late, close to 10 p.m. Sometimes I was the last person to leave the building, except for the custodian, a lean man of Asian ancestry about 60 years old.

I would usually see him cleaning the rooms or mopping the hallways. Though he did not speak English fluently, he was always cheerful, smiling, ready with a kind word. His light blue uniform was somehow always spotless, and he wore a matching cap that gave him an almost commanding air, subtly indicating that he was the man in charge.

His movements were relaxed yet precise; they imbued a ritual purity. After class, when I packed my books and prepared to exit the classroom, he might quietly come to the door and say hello. On entering, he proceeded to meticulously clean the chalkboard, first wetting it down with a sponge, and then, in slow, fluid, even strokes, would wipe it dry, intermittently stepping back to make sure that no streak marks remained.

Especially because he was an older man, I felt a bit awkward watching him clean the room, even though I knew it was his job. But my unrest would soon pass because there was something hypnotic and calming about how he moved and set the place back in order. I felt myself experiencing an inner catharsis as I watched him work. He handled everything so gently, carefully; he exhibited such a natural and straightforward "oneness" with his duties that whatever he did seemed refreshingly pure, honest, authentically real.

His wholesome richness reminded me of Zen and Sufi masters, who, perhaps like him, would take on jobs the world considered lowly, simply because they wanted to be free of worldly, artificial things. I thought of the Taoist disciple who said of his master, "He did not have to say anything; it was enough just to watch him sweep." Everyday chores could thus take on transcendental (even holy) significance if accomplished with one's entire being. In cleaning the room, in setting straight the desks and chairs, the custodian was, in his own way and in his own space, helping to order, purify, and positively transform the cosmos.

Custodian denotes "one entrusted with the care of a particular person and/or place." Certainly the caretaker I would periodically encounter after class was the consummate personification of this. His happy demeanour and conscientious work not only helped to make the classroom comfortable, but also seemed to clear the air of the stress that can accumulate in a high-powered academic setting where many thousands of careers (and lives) are routinely formed.

It may well be that the most important thing that helps a college run smoothly is accomplished in the quiet anonymity of the night, by attentive staff who do not lecture or attend council meetings, who do not seek scholastic or administrative acclaim, but in physical and even metaphysical ways consistently restore and sustain the learning environment, nurturing the classroom grounds as might the campus gardeners who regularly prepare the soil to receive seed, that new flowers may grow. God entrusts them with the hidden work so necessary for higher education to function.

Like God, custodians tend to labour invisibly, cleaning corridors, clearing paths, and preparing rooms for students to gather in peace and wisdom, that they might come to engage in the highest education, which is love.

Bougainvillea Blossoms

While meeting with Lax on Patmos, I befriended a number of
the isle's natives. Like my hermit friend, they had acquired their
own life wisdom over the years, a way of existing in balanced
harmony with Creator and cosmos. Lax himself commented on
this:

> If you say that the people on an island have found a way of
> living, are you saying that they have found "the Way"? ...
> "The Way," a way of life that works for everyone, every-
> where? In ten years of living on this particular island, this
> impression, in me, has not weakened, but strengthened. I
> do think that most people, even the children, know how
> to live on this island; to me, their tiniest action reveals the
> kind of Wisdom that guides them all....[66]

Patmos's reputation as being a kind of wisdom school stems
back to early Christian times. It was a place of retreat for those
seeking "the one thing needful" (Luke 10.42), that is, the Love
of God. Popularly known then as the "New Jerusalem," it was
a blessed site with a reputation for peace and holiness, owing to

S.T. GEORGIOU, 1997.

Outside the town of Chora, Patmos. After assembling the bagpipe with great care, the old man began to play a simple folk tune while his wife looked on.

its biblical association with St. John the Evangelist and Seer, the Apostle who regularly emphasized the pre-eminence of Agape. Sometimes referred to as the "Sanctuary of Love," it had a perennial way of attracting pilgrims in search of rejuvenation, as I too came to discover.

The island was (and continues to be) a type of remote, ascetic locale—mountainous, in many parts barren, and ringed by sea. A kind of monastic poverty (and simple, theocentric purity) exists on this rock populated by a mere 2,000 inhabitants, many of whom, in their own quiet ways, participate in the naturally rustic, "less is more" atmosphere. For two millennia, the isle has existed as a kind of refining workshop meant to steer the spiritually sensitive toward love, the one thing needful.

During one of my research trips to Patmos, at an evening party hosted in Chora, the highest village of the isle, I happened upon a happy couple in their mid-80s, both natives. They owned the building in which the party was taking place and lived on the lowest level, in a kind of sub-basement, too small, it seemed to me, for comfort. A visiting singer was renting the spacious quarters above, and had invited friends over for a midsummer celebration.

At some point in the festivities I stepped out onto the back porch and noticed the couple below. They were seated on a small veranda; their arms were around each other, and they were taking in the view of the hills and sea.

After exchanging hellos, they invited me down. Though I insisted that they remain seated, they both got up slowly, helping one another to rise, and treated me to a small glass of ouzo and quince. I learned that the husband still worked as a farmer (certainly his weathered skin and gnarly hands testified to this), while his wife minded the home. Because they appeared to be very much in love, I asked them what had kept them together, and what secrets they could tell me about living long and well.

At first, they looked at each other and began to laugh. Then the old man waved his arm and matter-of-factly said that there really was no secret to their enduring affection or longevity. "Things are as they are," he declared. "I know my wife and my wife knows me. We don't hide from each other. We don't ask each other lots of questions, we aren't anxious, running around all the time. Everything is open between us. We say our prayers and do our work. Most of the day I am outside, and she is inside, and when we unite, we enjoy our company, thanks be to God."

For a while they became silent and looked out over the fields, as if contemplating their many years together. Then the woman quietly said to her husband, "I've always liked how you are happy. You make me happy, too, even when I might not feel so."

He smiled, looking to the ground almost shyly. Then he abruptly rose and said, "Shall I play for our visitor some music?"

Her eyes lit up. "Oh yes, go get your bagpipe."

Within a few minutes he came back with a box, inside of which was a goat's bladder and some wooden reeds. He had made the instrument decades ago. After assembling it with great care, he began to play a simple folk tune that distinctly contrasted with the pop music faintly echoing from the party above.

As the old man played, closing his eyes, wholly absorbed in his melody, his wife began to tell me a few things about their life together. "It is true what he said," she began. "We have always lived simply, honestly. He works the earth, as best he can, and I take care of the house. When he comes home from the fields he always puts a flower behind my ear, then gives me *lahana* (greens) with which I make dinner. At night our worlds come together, and the next morning the dance starts all over again."

I thought of the relaxed rhythm of their lives. By day he sowed and reaped the blessings of the earth, and by night she cultivated them in her own way, preparing them for their mutual delight. Their shared affection was refreshingly innocent, almost child-like. And at the same time they had loved each other deeply through the years, intimately, planting their hearts into one another, without reserve. They both imbued a sense of thanks-giving and rustic contentment; their joy was born of compassion, honest work, and united faith.

The old man stopped playing and turned to us. "Is my wife tell-ing you wild stories about me?" he asked with a wide grin.

"No," I responded. "Only good things—good like the music you are playing. You are both very lucky to have found each other. Many people would love to have your peace and happiness."

He laid down his bagpipe and emphatically placed both hands on his knees. "Like I said, my boy, there's really nothing to it. If you want to live long and well, treat everything (especially those you love) like the vegetables and fruit growing in the field—give them water, help them grow. We have forgotten how much the land can teach us. Now remember, I'm just a farmer, but that's my advice."

"And it's good advice," I replied. "It reminds me of what Petros [the nickname by which the islanders knew Robert Lax] used to say: 'Turn jungle into garden without destroying a single flower.'"[67]

They both smiled at this, and the old man took up his bagpipe and continued to play while his wife tapped her foot in steady rhythm. After listening to the music for a while, I ventured to ask her why she and her husband were not living upstairs, where they could reside in far greater space and comfort; the top level offered so much more room than the tight accommodations below.

With a twinkle in her eye she motioned skyward and said, "We are getting ready to board the balloon. We do not need much now, only the good Lord, each other, and a view to share. You see, when the balloon comes, we can't be weighed down, otherwise we won't be able to fly."

Her wise and candid response reminded me of the *sadhus*, the elders of India who make it a point to detach themselves from worldly possessions so that when death arrives, they might attain a higher state of reincarnation. At the same time, I thought of the "weighing of the heart" ceremony in ancient Egyptian mythology, wherein the deceased's heart was placed opposite *Maat*, the deity of Truth, symbolized by a mere feather. If the dead person's heart was purified of material desires, the heart came to an even balance with the lightness of the feather, and the joyful individual went on into paradise.

While conversing with the couple, I heard someone shout my name upstairs, and decided, at long last, to return to the party. Before I left, they urged me to drink one more round of ouzo, after which they heartily embraced me.

As I walked away, I saw them reach out to a bougainvillea tree growing by the veranda and take fistfuls of blossoms. These they let go as they waved goodbye, sending into the air a shower of bright red petals.

It was beautiful and holy to see the blossoms flutter in the breeze and fall about the couple. They had meant it as an extended blessing, but to me, the colourful gesture happily celebrated their long and fruitful life together, and the enhancement of their love in the world to come.

Revelation

About 6:00 on a Sunday morning I was awakened by shouting. It sounded like it came from a few blocks up the street. I sat up in bed and determined that it wasn't exactly shouting, more like a loud proclamation, a declaration of some sort.

It was a quiet morning, so the words soon became audible. Strangely enough, they sounded biblical. To my astonishment, they were from the Revelation according to St. John:

> After this, I looked, and lo, in heaven, an open door! And the first voice, which I heard speaking to me like a trumpet, said, "Come up hither, and I will show you what must take place after this." At once I was in the Spirit, and lo, a throne stood in heaven, with One seated on the throne! And He who sat there appeared like jasper and carnelian, and round the throne was a rainbow that looked like an emerald.... (Rev. 4.1-3)

A shiver ran through me. I quickly moved to the window and saw a barefoot black youth, about fourteen or fifteen years old, thin and wiry. He was wearing a white tank top and ragged tan shorts; raised in his hands was the large open Bible from which he was reading. He made his way down the middle of the wide street with a slow, dignified gait, all the while proclaiming the Revelation with a loud and commanding voice, as might an experienced preacher.

Altogether it was eerie, considering my deep involvement with Patmos and theology in general. And it seemed surreal, like an apocalyptic wake-up call. Who was the youth who seemingly came out of nowhere, whose voice was "crying in the wilderness"?

When he had passed my house I went outside to see where he was heading. He continued down the long residential street leading to the sea. Apparently, he had begun reading the text some time earlier, because when I first heard him delivering it, he was already well into the book.

I went back inside and sat on my bed. I recalled a time when I was eight years old or so, living in the same house. At about the same hour of the morning, I awoke to hear a distant trumpet blast, and took it to be the last trumpet announcing the end of the world, the coming of the Messiah. Excitedly I ran to my parents' room to tell them that Jesus was on his way.

This time, the apocalyptic scenario seemed much more immediate and real. A youth in tattered clothing, appearing like a child messenger of God, was proclaiming the Revelation in such an intense manner that it felt as though Christ was speaking through him, and was, indeed, "coming soon!" (Revelation 22.20).

For a minute I wondered if it really was the end, and the powers of heaven were in the process of convening upon earth. I thought of what the Desert Fathers had said about the last day, how the light of divine love will radiate throughout creation and warm the lovers of God but burn the unloving and unfaithful. Consequently nothing shall be hidden from the inescapable light of heaven (Psalm 19.6).

This Almighty Light is thought to be love-oriented even when "burning" evildoers. For it is people who make the bright Love of God unbearable in themselves when they consciously draw away from original Agape. Divine love then becomes like a searing hell-fire, tormenting those who have sinned against love, and who never bothered to cultivate it in their souls. Thus the Light's ability to warm or burn will depend upon the good or evil natures of those who react with its consistent love. In essence, all there really is is love; how love shall ultimately transfigure us will depend upon how open we make our hearts.

And then I thought of the Orthodox monk St. Symeon the New Theologian. He also believed that at the Lord's Second Coming, only unrepentant evildoers will undergo a fiery and terrible ordeal because they will continue to deny the Eternal and Almighty Good from which they came. The righteous, on the other hand, will not experience a dramatic change, for having always been with God, and having ever loved him, they shall forever be with the God of Love.

I suddenly wondered if I had loved God deeply and consistently enough to be considered worthy of divine favour. Robert Lax once told me that when we pass on, we will be quietly asked by Jesus, "What did you love?"

As I was ruminating on these things, I began to faintly hear the same arresting voice reverberating somewhere in the distance. The barefoot messenger was now proceeding back up the street, still reading from Revelation!

Again I went to the window, shaking my head and wondering if it had all been a bizarre, unrelenting dream. Yet there he was, walking with the same solid and determined gait, measuredly striding with a processional rhythm, his loud voice echoing throughout the neighbourhood. Just as he passed my house, he finished the book.

> He who testifies to these things says,
> "Surely I am coming soon."
> Amen. Come, Lord Jesus!
> The grace of the Lord Jesus be with all the saints.
> Amen.

Once more I went outside to see where the youth was going. He now had the Bible raised over his head, and was walking in total silence up the long wide street, up Ocean Avenue, toward the rising sun. Still feeling as if I was drifting through a strange, convoluted dream, I stood there for a while, half-expecting to wake up at any moment. But with Bible raised, the youth kept on walking, and the morning sun kept on rising, and the new day—a Sunday—quietly began.

Again I wondered: What if the end of the world was now happening? What if the first light of the New Eden was already dawning? What if the righteous youth had just ushered in the beginning of everything? Then a poem by the Spanish writer Juan Ramon Jimenez came to mind.

I have a feeling
that my boat has struck,
down there in the depths,
against a great thing.
And nothing happens!
Nothing… Silence… Waves…
Nothing happens?
Or has everything happened,
and are we standing now,
quietly, in the new life?[68]

S.T. GEORGIOU, 2004.

Tunnel leading to the sea. Lower Ocean Beach, San Francisco.

The Further Shore

The half-naked body washed up at the far end of Ocean Beach, toward Pacifica. I had been walking alone when I found it. The corpse must have been spotted earlier, because in the distance I could see a paramedic crew ambling down a cliff.

These were the remains of a man, about 35 years old. He was quite lean, with heavily matted brown hair. His very white, blue-toned chest bore severe lacerations. Ragged jeans clung to his thin, bony legs. I could not see his face well because it was turned over, hidden in the sand. One arm was twisted beneath him; the other was slightly raised and rigid, pointing back to the waves.

It was my first raw (and unexpected) encounter with death. I had seen my father die, and one of my grandparents, but they had expired in the hospital, and their departures were antici-pated. Here, just after teaching my last class of the day, I was taking in the sun and sea, and suddenly there was death.

The image of the body stayed with me for weeks. Whenever I walked along the surf I thought of the dead man, and regularly sent out prayers to him. The shock of finding his corpse led me to reflect deeply on the nature of death, certainly not as a nihilistic end point, but as the transformative passage through which we inherit new life. I felt that I had found him not only to pray for his repose, but to contemplate the final journey that all of us will one day make, the transit leading out of this world and into the next.

I remember how young he seemed; he had gone to the "other side" early in life. It was impossible to tell exactly how—did he fall from a ship? Was he the victim of a crime? It is this "how" aspect of dying that troubles many of us. While the fact remains that everything living will die, no one knows how it will happen for them: through old age, accident, disease, injury, even violence. And it is this "how" part that accentuates the agony of losing a loved one. Why did this man have to perish this way, flung up on the shores of land's end? And why so young? Why was it his time to die?

When death comes, especially without warning, we are caught up in anguish. And yet our pain, though understandable, may keep us from communing with those who have gone on to paradise, and are with God. Our cries and torturous questions prevent us from sensing the calm waves of peace and love these souls incessantly extend throughout creation. For they carry memory of us in their beings, just as we do of them. Already a means of interdimensional communication exists: the spiritual wires are in place, linking this world with the next, but our emotional pain effects a bad connection. As St. Augustine said in his *Confessions*, the energy expended in mourning is better channelled through prayer.[69]

God knows our loved ones, both living and dead, better than we do. God's plans for them are far greater than anything we can ever conceive. The interconnected nature of reality (uniting this world and the next) is infinitely bigger than we can suppose. Therefore the Creator is not asking us to merely feel good in him, but *to trust him through love in every moment*, no matter what. All we have to do is believe and love. Though this injunction sounds simple, it is often the hardest thing in life to do.

Christ himself—the very incarnation of love—said, "Do not be afraid, only believe" (Mark 5.36). St. John the Divine put it another way: "Perfect love casts out fear" (1 John 4.18). St. Paul asserted, "Love hopes all things, believes all things, endures all things" (1 Corinthians 13.7). True believers freely allow God to work unconditionally throughout creation because they not only trust in the final cosmic outcome, but know that the Lord of Agape is wholly compassionate:

> Let not your hearts be troubled … in my Father's house are many rooms; if it were not so, would I have told you that I go to prepare a place for you? (John 14.1-2). For I am the resurrection and the life; those who believe in me, though they die, shall live (John 11.25). For this is the will of my Father, that those who see the Son and believe in him should have eternal life; and I will raise them up on the last day (John 6.40).

Christ promises us these things because without him, nothing in this life is certain. We live in an imperfect, fallen world, altered since the time of Adam. While our spirits are eternal, our bodies, like all living things, are fragile. Pascal, the seventeenth-century scientist turned theologian, rightly said, "A drop of water [if tainted with a pathogen] can kill a man."[70] It is something of a miracle that we continue to thrive in such a precarious realm of potential chaos and imminent dissolution. Since this is the case, we do well not to focus our spiritual energies on how and when we will die (for we can perish through any means at any given time), but on transcending death through the love of Jesus. The power that effected the Resurrection (and the original Creation) will one day raise us up and transfigure the cosmos.

Each day, the same questions about death are being asked all over the world. There are no easy answers, because the human mind cannot fathom the great mystery in which we live. We are poised between the natural and supernatural worlds. Things that happen here affect what is happening there, and things generated there affect what is transpiring here, all in ways and patterns that we can hardly understand. Our perception of the complex mystery surrounding us is akin to an elementary knowledge of sunlight. Initially, we think it to be nearly colourless, but if we hold up a prism, we see that all the colours of the rainbow are invisibly contained in the light. Wavelengths of light are extremely subtle, like God's presence in our living, dying, and ultimate rebirth.

Because the same questions pertaining to the end of life are routinely being voiced everywhere, we cannot think of the loss of a loved one as happening only to us; everyone is going through a similar pain. The whole world is burning. And yet out of the fire has come Christ, the God who also suffered and died and then rose from the dead in a very real way, ensuring the collective transfiguration of creation. "Do you have wounds?" Christ will ask. "Look at mine." And with hands bearing the marks of the nails, he will restore our broken hearts and lift us out of the death of this world and into the life of the next.

Still though, some may ask, why do we have to die at all? Because we are alive. Because, like seeds, we must break open to bloom elsewhere. Because unless we die, we cannot live in a greater, more complete, and perfected body. As Jesus said, "Unless a grain of wheat falls into the ground and dies, it remains alone. But if it dies, it produces much grain" (John 12.24).

Simply put, we die because God died for us, clearing a path for our own transformation. As disciples we follow the Lord unto death, that we may rise with him. This is the central concept of the New Testament—the Good News—that though we die, we live again in the glory of the Risen Christ. And when we resurrect in Jesus, our lives will at last be complete. We will have ended one phase of spiritual becoming, that we may begin another. For Christ is the renewing centre toward which all things gravitate, the Almighty God who said, "I will draw all peoples to Myself" (John 12.32).

Strangely enough, we Christians are already dead and already risen. This is so because we participate in the sacraments of a God who long ago conquered death. The very fact that we gather and celebrate God *here*, indicates that one day we shall assemble and praise God *there*. As members of the communal Body of Christ, we already are "there," but the veil of this life must fall for us to completely behold our Beloved, who is radiating everywhere at once. And yet there are moments when we feel the presence of God so acutely that it seems as if we have, even now, crossed over to the further shore.

Chief Seattle, a well-known elder of the Duwamish, a Native American tribe of the northwest, once said, "There is no death, only a change of worlds."[71] In light of the eternity of love, and our infinite progress through it, the idea of a deathless transition rings true, and hearkens of *theosis*. We say that we die, but deep in our hearts, we know that death is simply one of many never-ending transits leading to (and through) a God who is forever. From baptism on, we are steadily being grafted into a holy body of love that will ensure our immortality and eternal salvation. This "Agape Body" is without limitations, without end; and we, as products of it—and spiritual participants in it—can never perish, only mysteriously transform from glory unto glory (Philippians 3.21). For like the God of love who is undying, so anything born of God's love will never know death.

But what exactly will heaven be like? Will we reunite with our loved ones from whom we were separated so long ago? Will we once more embrace everyone who loved us and helped us on our journey?

On this topic, Robert Lax wrote in his journal: "I remember the people I loved, those who have died or have just disappeared—I remember their traits as though it were a sacred duty. What possible use for all those memories unless we were, somehow, all to meet again?"[72]

Surely if life (born of love) is holy, then nothing in creation will be lost, whether material or spiritual. Matter and Spirit came into being through love, and in love they shall once more fuse and renew themselves. All things in creation have a deep inter-affinity, a kind of undying memory of their common origin because life issued from the same Source. And God Almighty does not forget what came into existence through him; even now we live and make sense of the cosmos only because we participate in a supernatural consciousness, a wisdom and intelligence consistently emanating compassion.

In all creatures, and especially in us, there is a single unchanging power, and this is the presence of love, the mystery that will make every atom, cell and fibre wholly and inconceivably new. Thus God said to a multitude of dried bones strewn in the desert—the remains of a great army—"I will lay sinews upon you, and will cause flesh to come upon you, and cover you with skin, and put breath in you, and you shall live; and you will know that I am the Lord" (Ezekiel 36.6).[73]

On the nature of our imminent resurrection and transit into the afterlife, St. Paul exclaimed, "God has prepared, for those who love Him, things beyond our seeing, beyond our hearing, beyond our imagining" (1 Corinthians 2.9). Likewise, he also said, "Who hopes for what he sees?" (Romans 8.24). Should anyone be told of the wonders of paradise and the unprecedented splendour of the renewed creation, they would not believe it. It would be like telling someone who had no understanding of modern science that tiny microscopic cells make up the human body, or that matter can be reduced to (and beyond) atomic structure. We require another form of existence and perception—our *resurrection body*—to better comprehend the glory and infinite magnitude of Eden reborn.

Every one of us will be resurrected. We will hear the gentle, reverberating Voice that shall call all things back into existence. We will hear our names whispered with such great intensity and love that we shall stir into a new waking, an unprecedented state of being. We will not forget the old world, but shall see what we could not clearly see before: that, ever since the beginning, we were created to be co-participants of joy, faithful lovers of life. And even if, at times, we were not, or did not feel so, we shall happily discover how that joy continued to have faith and love in us; otherwise, we would never have been born.

On the further shore, blood will become fire, and fire will become light. We will take our rightful place among the stars and ride eternity with the angels. At the throne of the King we will rediscover the open secret of the universe: that love is really all there is—a simple truth, but one that takes a lifetime to comprehend, and is ultimately realized in the presence of the loving Master. His eyes and ours shall meet, and we will see for the first time.

One spring morning, after I drove to campus, I remained in my car and began thinking about relatives and friends who had recently passed away, including the man I had found on the beach. I wondered where they were, if they were happy. All at once a great gust of wind arose, and the cherry tree beneath which I had parked let loose a flood of blossoms that covered my windshield. Again and again the wind blew, each time releasing yet more blossoms, wave after wave after wave.

    Love
    waves
    always,
    all
    ways[74]

    Robert Lax

Breath by Breath

One mid-morning, while gathering research for my dissertation
at the Robert Lax Archives in New York, I found a handwritten
poem of his that made me more aware of my breathing.

in
in
out

in
in
out

breathe
in
breathe
in

breathe
out
breathe
out

in
in
out[75]

It came to me that much of life moves according to this in-out cycle. There is inflow, and there is outflow, a vital, incessant process mirroring the endless contraction-expansion of the cosmos. Waves, tides, the day-night sequence, flowers that open at dawn and close at dusk, the human heartbeat—a certain ingoing and outgoing rhythm pulses in creation. Moreover, inflow is ever transforming into outflow, both in the inhalation-exhalation process and in the dynamic flux of the universe. This constant change is the defining principle of existence, insuring its continuity.

Living things, then, may be said to move with a steady beat, a kind of rhythmic uniformity; the earth itself spins, and is in cyclic transit. Even the Holy Trinity may be described as a perpetual flow leading from the Father, to the Son, to the Spirit. As kinetic creatures, we too are constantly in motion, absorbing and releasing energy; we share the animating spark of the universe, the catalytic fire of God breathed into humanity since Adam.

Whatever lives, therefore, endures not by remaining static, but by changing ceaselessly. As the Pre-Socratic Heraclitus said, "Change is the principle of all things that exist; we cannot step into the same river twice." Likewise, Taoism sums up this philosophy in its popular yin-yang symbol. *Yin* (the cosmic force representing the feminine, dark, night, earth) perpetually moves in tandem with its opposite, *yang* (interpreted as masculine, light, day, heaven). Yin and yang remain in never-ending flux because they seek to attain an eternal goal: universal equilibrium.

As many philosophical and spiritual systems have made evident, divine energy is ever in motion, a flow most intimately exemplified in our rhythmic breathing. Interestingly, the ceaseless inflow-outflow of human respiration may be likened to our ongoing (and infinite) movement toward the very source of life. We will ever be entering and exiting "the many mansions of our Father's house" (John 14.2) as we travel through eternity toward the Almighty, learning more as we proceed from "glory unto glory" (2 Corinthians 3.18). Certainly the daily (or weekly) rhythm of entering and exiting church each Sunday prefigures this everlasting soul trek.

In their yogic (breath-body) studies, Indian mystics rendered a maxim that has enduring interfaith value: "In the daily breaths that we take live the secrets that the masters have been trying to teach us." This foundational belief is enhanced when we consider that each inhalation and exhalation is something like a birth and a death—an entry into this life *(inflow)*, and an exit into the next *(outflow)*. Thus with every mindful breath we recreate ourselves, and, at the same time, prepare for our impending transit into heaven.

When we inhale, it is as if we are born into this world, taking on the fullness of life; when exhaling, we let go this realm, emptying ourselves of it. *Inflow* may be likened to what we come to know of creation—for us, living is an increasingly ascertainable experience. *Outflow* leads us back into the mystery of God from which we came—an increasingly transcendent return.

In a way, inhalation and exhalation are like two interrelated halves of a greater whole—a consummate circle of being. The first half of this vital circumference begins with *inhalation* and then transforms, in the second half, into *exhalation*. When the cycle is complete, a pneumatic round is formed, a completed ring of respiration, of life. Thus in one breath, we mystically unite our beginning and our end, as well as the realms of earth and heaven.

Via our God-given, theocyclic breaths, it may be said that we ride the rhythms of God's spirit-energy into the great beyond. Who knows if the 23,000 breath-cycles we complete each day will altogether, over a lifetime, form a kind of swirling immaterial vortex or hyperphysical tunnel through which we shall enter the next existence? Perhaps through our daily respirations (or re-*spirations*) we will one day spiral (spirate) on toward some greater, increasingly holy dimension.

Breath is energy, shared grace, the pneumatic spark of life and consciousness, animating humanity since Adam. Indeed, the very atoms of air that once passed through the lungs of Adam (and those of the prophets and saints, Mother Mary, and Christ himself) are now coursing through ours, in some way sanctifying us as we approach the God of love from which we came.

All in all, breath is the blessed Spirit-Wind that allows us to move through the holy flux of life, riding the infinite wave-flows of eternity. As faithful waveriders, we are meant to do so calmly, trusting in the greater cosmic design. We do not hold onto each breath, but let them go by, confident that another will come. In essence, we relax, we have faith in the flow, and go with it, spiriting our way through the ins and outs of earth and heaven, breath by breath. Our present breaths breathe in our life of tomorrow.

On the cyclic wave-rhythms of life, breath, and creation, Robert Lax, while living and working with the poor in Marseilles, wrote the following poem shortly after discovering an icon of St. John

the Divine in his hotel room. He took this as a mystical sign
indicating that he should journey to Patmos, the holy isle that
would become his spiritual and creative home:

> the tale
> is like
> a spider's
> web
> spun out
> and swallowed
> in
>
> the tale
> the tale
> a silver
> thread
> spun out
> and swallowed
> in...[76]

Indivisible Agape

During a celebration of the Divine Liturgy at the St. Demetrios Greek Orthodox Chapel in Berkeley, I heard the priest say this emphatic prayer while preparing holy communion:

> The Lamb of God is broken and distributed,
> broken but not sundered,
> always fed upon but never consumed...

These words are a regular part of the Communion Anthem of St. John Chrysostom (fourth century), said every Sunday in the Eastern Church, but it was as if I had heard them for the first time. Their power made a deep impression on me. The Lamb of God is indeed indivisible and inexhaustible, even though his Holy Body is ritually "broken" unto eternity. And while he is certainly our spiritual sustenance, Christ is impossible to consume, owing to his infinite, almighty nature.

This mystery directly affects all followers of Christ as well. As members of his living Soma, we too will ever remain whole, intact, even though the trials of life may "break" us, and death shall ultimately tear us from this world. For as baptized believers, we have become part of a greater Body in whom, through whom, for whom we live, that our physical and spiritual natures may be ultimately restored to their original theocentric glory—a pre-Fall state free of decay and death, exuding life and joyous rapture. At that time, all created things will reflect the united love of God without end.

Already we have evidence of this impending transfiguration; already there are signs indicating that life in the resurrected Saviour is (and will ever be) unbroken. Paradoxically, this wholeness is demonstrated in *reliquiae* (the bones of the saints, many fragmented and reduced to mere shards), which are often found to be fragrant, luminous, healing, even able to restore the dead to life, according to Scripture (2 Kings 13.21).

Icon of Jesus above the altar in the Chapel of St. Demetrios, Patriarch Athenagoras Orthodox Institute, Berkeley (Thomas Doolan, Iconographer).

CHRISTOPHER JOHN ROZALES, 2006.

Like Jesus, saints allow their body to be "broken for the life of the world" because they know that the animating energy exuding from their bones is (and has always been) God's—the same irreducible power that illumined their heart in the first place. Infused with this holiness, saints realize that death does not sunder them from their almighty life source, but makes them spiritually stronger. They have already gone over to the other side and long to confer blessings from there to here, from the Creator to creation.

Through their sanctified bodily remains (which on the last day will be resurrected and reunited with their souls—a psycho-biological restoration mirroring the impending harmony of heaven and earth), saints radiate the intact and undying love of Christ throughout the universe. A great peace and warmth emanates from relics because the bright spirits once enfleshed in them ardently anticipate the transfiguration of the cosmos, the transformation of the physical and spiritual worlds into something entirely new. Therefore saints throughout time ecstatically and inexhaustibly sing with us:

Christ is born,
Christ is risen,
Christ will come again.

Many intuitive Christians feel an indescribable sweetness in the presence of holy relics. They perceive divine energy alive in them, swirling like heaven's breath in the hollows of their marrow. They innately sense the Lamb of God stirring deep in their lacunae, beyond the infinite recesses of their very atoms, for even now the Light of the world is preparing for the ultimate deification of our souls and bodies.

Relics speak to believers. In them the faithful recognize an original, eternal, and salvific power "broken and distributed, broken but not sundered," a transcendent life lighting its way through flesh and blood, psyche and spirit, that all living things may be restored in Love, and enjoy communion with their bright Lord anew.[77]

Good Vibrations

It had been an arduous day. My GTU classes began in the early morning and ended about 10 p.m., with a gruelling midterm exam. After a late dinner with fellow students, I raced over to the downtown subway station and caught the last train going back to San Francisco.

Only a half-dozen people were on board the midnight car. Some slept, some listened to their headphones in zombie fashion; others read the newspaper, news already a day old.

A few stops later, three teenage girls boarded the train. They were shouting and laughing, making a nuisance of themselves, which was especially disturbing those trying to sleep. But after a while the trio quieted down and, of all things, began to sing! First, one girl hummed a long mellow note, with which the others harmonized, then all three joined in a stirring Gospel tune praising "the Lord Almighty."

It was a wonderful surprise, both spiritually and aesthetically, like a blessing from above. Their melodic voices were soothing, calming, vibrantly deep, then high and ethereal. Passengers broke into smiles and happily listened. Everyone relaxed and took in the show.

It was amazing to see how the impromptu performance inspired the riders to suddenly become friendly with the girls and each other. Psychic walls had broken down; the music had changed everyone for the better.

Restful melodies—ranging from Gregorian and Tibetan chants to classical symphonies and synthesizer music—are being given scientific credit for reducing stress, minimalizing pain perception, bolstering the immune system, and helping to improve memory and I.Q. There is a definitive connection between what we hear and how we feel. Sound affects us so strongly because our bodies are 70 percent water, which makes them optimum conductors of subtle and overt vibrations. We hear both with our ears and with our very cells. Quite literally, we are beings hard-wired to tune in and resonate.

Pythagoras, the famous pre-Socratic philosopher, believed that everything that is alive (not only birds, whales, and people) has the capacity to sing. Validating his claim, some geneticists have identified musical patterns in the DNA of many living creatures, from microscopic organisms to humans. Even pulsing stars and galaxies seem to emit rhythmic, tonal vibrations, leading some scientists to believe that a type of underlying melodic pattern—a harmonic frequency that the whole of life responds to—may govern the entire cosmos. Interestingly, the early Hindus believed that the original sound of the universe (which all living things are subconsciously said to emit) is *om*. According to the *Vedas*, the physical, mental, and spiritual worlds, as well as the waking, dream, and sleep states, may be compressed into this single mystic syllable.

As I was ruminating on these things and listening to the talented singers on the subway, two rough-looking, heavily muscled men bolted aboard at the Twelfth Street Station. An immediate energy shift took place in the car. Tension and fear had replaced a shared sense of peace. The hostility of the pair cut through the air like a knife, and it seemed obvious that they did not mean well.

And yet the girls kept on singing. I saw them glance at the men with faint smiles, and went right on with their hymn. This unexpected reaction may have addled the toughs (as did the Gospel music in itself), because following their malicious entry, there was a noticeable hesitation on their part to do anything. They looked around in what seemed to be an unsure, near-helpless manner, a mounting uncertainty that the singers and onlooking riders quickly perceived.

The girls then raised their voices. A few of the passengers joined in the spiritual song, clapping their hands and belting out the refrain, "Hallelujah!" We all started to feel a powerful sense of solidarity. Within minutes, the two men stormed out of the car at the West Oakland Station, after which everyone broke into applause and laughter.

Later, as I was walking home in the clear and quiet spring darkness, taking in the stars overhead, Pythagoras again came to mind. Not only did he believe that planetary bodies (and all things) are alive in song, he also felt that the spiritually purified can hear the united music of creation, a universal hymn so perfect and celestial he termed it "The Music of the Spheres."

This rarefied music is the very harmony of God. This is the mystic melody of life, the Life within life. This is the love song of Heaven, ever-reverberating from the invisible wires that have strung the cosmos together since its genesis.

If we could but hear that ecstatic music, tune into its supernatural, rhapsodic sound, then anything and everything would become possible because it would be the stellar symphony of what *Is*. We would move magically, without limitations, because we would vibrate at the pitch of the eternal, in perfect sync with the Holy Spirit. Ultimately, we would return to our celestial source and flow wherever life's song would take us.

> He began to whistle a tune from the depths of his soul. He had never heard it before but he recognized it as a form of the song his soul had always been singing, a song he had been singing since the beginning of the world, a song of return. It was as though he stood in a dark corner of the universe and whistled softly, between his teeth, and the far stars were attentive, as though he whistled and waves far off could hear him, as though he had discovered a strain, at least, of the night song of the world.

> Robert Lax, from *Circus of the Sun*[78]

Iconwork

While in graduate school, I periodically exhibited my icons locally. One in particular, the *Blue Madonna*, continues to have special significance for me. It was created in a style I termed "Neo-Byzantine Folk Art." This type of iconography makes use of acrylics (instead of traditional egg tempera) and materials derived from nature. Even bits of debris, found by chance along the roadside, may be utilized in this mixed media style.

I began work on *Blue Madonna* during one of my research trips to Patmos. While wandering through various chapels, I found myself studying icons of Mary, and occasionally sketching them. At the same time, I began collecting small pieces of broken glass, stone, and metal en route to these shrines, hopeful that one day I would make an icon of Mary using materials that society had deemed valueless. It seemed to me that these simple items could add a kind of rustic charm to the Marian image that was slowly forming in my mind.

On returning to San Francisco, I continued gathering "useless" objects that I chanced upon, particularly along Ocean Beach. Twisted wire, glass shards, tile fragments, copper scraps, wave-worn shells and stones, and driftwood made up the foundational design. Eventually, *Blue Madonna* came into being. The image illustrates the poverty of Mother Mary (hence the liberal use of insignificant items), who, like her nomadic Son, had "nowhere to lay her head," and emptied her heart of self-centred pursuits in order to willingly become the *Theotokos*, or God-Bearer. And like Jesus, she underwent a second self-emptying, this time at the Crucifixion, when she was utterly divested of her Son.

Blue Madonna depicts Mary singly, without the Christ child, a periodic theme in Orthodox iconography. Here she takes on a more authoritarian image and is visualized as the Protectress of the Faithful. Noble, mature, almost stern, Mary not only reflects on the passion of her Son, but simultaneously displays the instrument of his death (the cross) in the form of a neck medallion flanked by two small metallic fish. And yet while the Holy Mother quietly meditates on the magnitude of Jesus' sacrifice, radiant stones, bright arcs of copper, and life-affirming blue and green tones shine around her, indicating that Jesus' immolation will inevitably yield light and universal salvation. Mary's austere expression consequently hints of a subtle sweetness, a sorrow steadily gladdening.

Like the driftwood on which the icon is created, the shells and beach stones give a predominant oceanic feel to the image. The sea association is suggestive of the eternal and fathomless mystery of God out of which life is born and into which life is baptized. The sea symbolically hearkens of Jesus, both as the Fish and the Great Fisherman.

Isidore of Seville, a sixth-century bishop and theologian, relates that Mary's name denotes "Star of the Sea."[79] The waters of the deep therefore may also be likened to the divine embryonic fluid of the cosmos, a distinctly feminine image whose archetype is Mary, the Bearer, Life-Sustainer, and divinely chosen Nurturer of Jesus. Small wonder that many of the early Church fathers referred to Mary as the "Ark of Christ."

The *Blue Madonna*'s association with the sea is profoundly environmental and organic. Indeed, an inseparable link exists between the Mother of Christ and the entire cosmos, because it is through the body of Mary (in this case, *the human microcosm*) that God took on flesh and began to resanctify the universe (*the collective macrocosm*). When the Holy Spirit "overshadowed" Mary and she conceived Christ, the supernatural event consequently linked her with all of physical matter—the "greater body" of life. Understood in this light, Mary may be regarded as Mother Nature (or, more accurately, as the Mother of Re-Sanctified Nature), the Queen not only of a new heaven, but of a new earth as well.

In making this icon, I remember the spiritual and creative impact that "Mary as macrocosm" had upon me, for in addition to the "Cosmic Christ" (the Incarnated Son), there is also the "Cosmic Mary." Through her the Good News and life in the new Eden came into tangible fruition. This new life was first generated in the womb of Mary, the sourcepoint of paradise reborn and the fount from which the transfigured cosmos issues. It is for this very reason that the Madonna's predominant colour is blue, reflective of the sky which, like a womb, encircles everything, and is the sum of all. In a sense, the whole of life is contained in Mary's "cosmic and celestial womb," waiting to be entirely "born again" in Christ.

Like Christ, Mary then is a mediator, the all-holy link between heaven and earth, the Mother of Salvation, the Altar of the Church, the blessed Handmaid of Redemption who through her love and faith brought Almighty Love into the world. The energy of this supernatural birth was akin to the explosion of the Big Bang that created the universe. Mary's womb contained the great seed of the new genesis, the organic spark of the God-Man, the "Light of the Logos" through whom all things are steadily being remade, just as they were originally brought to fruition in the beginning, when "all things were created through him" (John 1.3).

Thus in the *Blue Madonna*, radiant stones, tile and glass swirl around Mary the Light-Bearer. And in bearing Jesus, Our Lady herself became eternally possessed of light, totally effulgent, wholly divine, the Candle of Grace and Mercy "whom all generations would call blessed" (Luke 1.48).

When polishing and laying in the bright sea-stones, I prayed myself into the work and sought out the blessings of the Mother of Life. Quietly, reverently, I longed to transmute the awesome majesty of nature into the icon. Sun and sky, clouds and wind, the wave-swept sea (and the creatures therein)—all of it I consciously dedicated to Mary, Queen of the Cosmos. In essence, I tried to become something like an "open vessel" through which divine energy might flow. And then I considered how Mary, in an incomparably holy way, had, through grace, become the supreme creative channel when she gave her wholehearted assent to the Power of the Most High and said, "Let it be according to thy will" (Luke 1.38).

This "Yes of faith"—which we all give when we place our trust in a greater design—is indeed the beginning of everything, both spiritually and creatively. We let go of ego and calculative intent and allow the rhythm of the Spirit to take over. The mind relaxes and becomes like a clear window through which light passes, infusing a tranquil, joyous warmth into the house of the soul.

Making an icon involves a similar process. Like Mary, the spiritual artist steadily forgets himself, becoming conscious only of the "now moment" and its infinite power. His mind enters his heart, and he floats in a timeless, holy present. Quietly, almost imperceptibly, he becomes an instrument of a higher purpose, in the process realizing that everything in creation is an icon meant to reveal the glory of God.

When the *Blue Madonna* was taken to the Annunciation Greek Orthodox Cathedral in San Francisco for installation, a priest read prayers of consecration over it and blessed the image with holy water from both Patmos and Lourdes, empowering its ability to function as a vessel of grace. It was then set on a chair while the workmen and I went into an adjoining room to gather various tools. When we returned, we found the icon in the arms of an elderly woman who had wandered into the church. She held it like a baby and repeatedly kissed it, saying, "Mary, Mary, Mother of Christ!"

A smile spread across my face as she cradled and revered the icon. Its inner doors had suddenly and blessedly opened, perhaps even through the Handmaid of God.

Hail Mary, full of grace! Hail *Panaghia Theotokos*, All-Holy Mother of the Lord!

"Blue Madonna," by S.T. Georgiou. Annunciation Greek Orthodox Cathedral, San Francisco.

Desert Secret

During the summer months, friends of Lax—mostly European writers and artists—would visit him, if only to have quiet evening walks with the poet along the waterfront. Simply through spending a few hours in his happy, loving presence, they found themselves becoming more wise and compassionate people. (Thomas Merton once said of Lax that he "was born with an inborn direction to the living God,"[80] while Jack Kerouac, another early admirer, affectionately nicknamed him "Laughing Buddha."[81])

One of Lax's regular visitors was Gianvito (Vito) Lo Greco, from Rome. He and I had made our acquaintance on Patmos during the summer I met Lax, 1993, and we quickly became good friends.

Vito had worked as an air traffic controller when he first came to the holy isle. A flamboyant 30-year-old, he arrived with his Honda Golden Wing, then the most luxurious of motorcycles, a 1500-cc "Anniversary Edition Special" complete with two rear stereos. I would see him cruising around the harbour sporting a bright red neckerchief, riding gloves, and aviator sunglasses, and wondered if he might be a movie star or some wealthy European playboy.

But then, one afternoon, by the pier, I saw him deeply engrossed in the *Tao Te Ching (The Way and Its Power,* the foundational classic of Taoism). We began to talk, and I learned that he was

The Italian artist Gianvito Lo Greco, S.T. Georgiou, and the 1500 cc Honda Golden Wing. Port of Skala, Patmos.

MARKUS ROETZER, 1993.

going through the beginnings of some type of spiritual transformation. He had become increasingly interested in the nature of God, and how God may be expressed through art.

In the days that followed, during a seaside walk with Lax, I introduced Vito to the "Poet of Patmos." Something told me that he could help Vito in his spiritual and artistic awakening, just as the sage had recently inspired me in my own inner journey.

Lax had an immediate rapport with the young Italian. He encouraged him to pursue his artistic interests, believing that these would assist him in his soul-searching. The poet had always felt that creating and praying were two sides of the same coin.

Shortly thereafter, Vito began to adopt an increasingly minimalist (less is more) lifestyle. He gave up his job as an air traffic controller and entered an art academy in Rome. Eventually he began to exhibit his work. One of these shows took place on Patmos, which Lax attended and thoroughly enjoyed. Lax had once told me that the emerging artist's upbeat energy reminded him of Thomas Merton—they both had a similar walk, he said, as if firecrackers were exploding under their feet.

In my conversations with Vito, I learned that Lax had helped him see how, for both the artist and the monk, the primary goal is to empty the self of all that is selfish, egoistic, and turbulent in order to make room for the Spirit of God, the underlying Essence of All. Whether we are making art or praying, we must aim to open our hearts as much as possible, that the original light of creation may shine through us. If the real canvas is life, and everyone is a brush of God, the best way to flow with the

Artist is to relax and move with him, and with the universe, his holy masterwork.

Naturally, this way of spiritual and expressive living does not come about through rigorous intellectualization and lengthy dialogue, but via a kind of silent detachment, a meditative waiting on God that is familiar to mystics. The self is emptied of all excesses, superficialities, and social conditioning; this purgative contemplation or *kenosis* ultimately leads to a quiet state of nothingness. Herein, the hidden God—limitless and incomprehensible—can be waited for only in the silence of self-surrender and unknowing.[82] It is, in essence, an intuitive and heart-centred way of preparing oneself to receive the divine mystery, the almighty Power who, at his discretion, breaks through the void in love.

Some years after meeting Lax, Vito had a profound spiritual encounter. In many ways, it seemed to experientially echo what Lax had helped him to understand, or better put, rediscover in himself. It took place in the desert, near Israel. For many months he would not speak of his "Desert Secret," as he termed it. Then finally, after visiting me in San Francisco, he wrote a moving letter describing what had taken place. Its contents, printed with his permission, follow.

September 4, 1998

Dear Steve–

Sorry for my delay, but I was waiting for the right time to tell you about "Desert Secret."

One thing has to be clear—even though I write to you about this, and we may speak of this, everybody must experience their own "Desert Secret." It could be in the Desert, on Ocean Beach in San Francisco, in the Himalayas, on Patmos, but what's important is the personal experience. Books, talking, rationality, information, knowledge about the world and all things in it, they are nothing, really.

Steve, you wrote some very nice letters to me since I left San Francisco, good and long letters, and I thank you for your thoughts. You know and understand many things. But "Desert Secret" doesn't need so many words. Let me explain.

While I was in Israel, I was at a place called Masada. From a high terrace, I looked out over the red-gold "Negev" (the Desert), and He was calling me. So I took the motorbike and rode for 70 kilometres. As I went up a hill, I felt I had to stop the engine, sit on a rock, and be quiet. Up there I heard the silence, the wind, the voice of the Desert, and He told me simply, "Look at me—I Am. There is nothing more—*I Am.*" And I started to cry.

And the Desert told me His Secret which is a "Secret without a secret." He told me what I always knew. He told me that there is nothing left to do in this life except discover the Life within, the "Being" that we all have inside of us ever since we were born. This is real wisdom. It seems simple, but we forget this wisdom quite soon.

Then, after I left that place, I was riding between the Desert and the Dead Sea, and there was this powerful sunset. There was nobody around, only the very strong landscape, the colours, and the silence. For a while there was no difference between me and what was around me. My mind exploded into thousands and thousands of pieces, I saw its pure nature—I felt God, and Love. I cried again, but this time for a long, long time. I couldn't stop. And I said thanks.

Now you know the "Desert Secret." But as I told you, speaking about it is only a little thing. The experience is most important. And not only this, but to keep the experience alive for the rest of your life. This is the biggest and most difficult step.

Love from the Depth of my Heart,

Much Peace to you always,

Your Spiritual Brother,
Gianvito

Water and Light

On one of my summer trips to Patmos, I was invited by a monk to witness a baptism that was to take place near a shoreline monastery. The man being baptized, from California and of no prior religious faith, was soon to marry a Patmian woman who had helped him convert to Christianity. The ceremony was to be performed in the ancient manner, that is, via full immersion into a living body of water, meaning flowing water, as in a river or sea.

Not only was it rare to see an adult baptism in the Eastern Orthodox Church; it was even rarer for the sacrament to be conducted outdoors, in direct contact with the beauty of nature, according to the old rite. Moreover, in Orthodoxy, all the sacraments of Christian initiation—Baptism, Chrismation (called Confirmation in the Western tradition), and Holy Communion—are conducted in a single tri-part service. For a believer like me, the highly colourful and renewing experience would be like reliving my own baptism.

S.T. GEORGIOU, 1993.

Bay of St. Loukas, Patmos. The two priests bent down, touched the man on the head and shoulders, and fully immersed him three times into the sea, baptizing him "in the name of the Father, and of the Son, and of the Holy Spirit."

At about 10 a.m., I made my way down to the radiant cove where the ceremony was to be held. Around 30 guests, mostly family, had congregated by the waterside, waiting for the initiate and clergy to come out of the castle-like monastery. Steps from the rear of the courtyard led down to a small stone pier. This was the path of rebirth soon to be taken by the neophyte.

First the elaborately robed priests came out and approached a small seaside table, on which lay holy books and vessels used in conducting the rite. The three clerics spanned youth, mid-life, and old age: one priest was very old, with a flowing white beard and hair wound in a bun; the other was middle-aged, almost a younger version of the older. Following them was a deacon in his 20s who carried a candle and censer.

At last came the catechumen, accompanied by two novice monks. I was surprised to see that he was not a young man, but a fellow about 60. He wore shorts and a simple white gown with a cross embroidered on the back, and was barefoot. When he reached the pier, he was embraced by his fiancée, a tranquil-looking woman about the same age, and they exchanged the kiss of peace.

After reading initial prayers renouncing Satan and affirming allegiance to Christ, the priests sang hymns to bless and consecrate the waters. The elder priest signed the sea thrice with a large Byzantine-style cross whose polished gold sharply reflected the sun's rays.

An intense quiet then came over the members of the congregation, as they knew that the neophyte was soon to be immersed. The clergy's chanting added to the peace, as did the birds singing in the nearby trees. All the while, the sweet smell of incense permeated the air.

Reaching over to the table, the elder priest took a glass vial containing the Oil of Gladness (blessed olive oil). Raising it to the sky, he explained that it is symbolic of *light* (in biblical times it was used to light lamps), *life* (it was commonly used in healing), and *peace* (as when the dove brought Noah the olive branch after the Flood). Then he moved over to the edge of the pier and poured the flask into the sea, making the sign of the cross three times with the holy oil, readying the waters—as God had once readied creation—to receive a new child of God, a new Adam.

As the oil fell into the deep, anointing the sea, I noticed something remarkable take place. From the point where the oil made initial contact with the water, the resultant layer of film, bright and rainbow-coloured, spread out like an ever-expanding "V" across the sea's surface, dissipating after about ten metres or so.

When oil meets water, irregular patches of the two fluids usually form, but in this case, arc after expanding arc of scintillating oil rippled over the wavelets. When I asked the woman next to me if she had noticed the phenomenon, she simply replied, "All kinds of miracles happen here; it is the power of Christ, the Angels, and St. John!"

I could only nod my head in spiritual solidarity. Judging by what I had witnessed, some kind of supernatural "pass-over" had indeed transpired, a paranormal manifestation of the divine presence, much like "the Spirit of God moving over the face of the waters" (Genesis 1.2).

Within minutes, the neophyte had descended the stone-hewn steps leading into the sea and stood before the priests, steadying himself in waist-high water. The elder priest looked at him intently, then gazed out over the entire congregation. In a loud voice that echoed throughout the cove, the aged man of God, looking like a biblical prophet, raised his arms toward heaven and said:

> As Christians we follow Jesus into the Jordan. As Christians we go down into the depths and die with our God, that we may rise with Him unto New Life and Light. As Christians we come to Christ cleansed, transfigured, and vested in Robes of Glory. So we descend into this water, that in it, we may meet with the Form that is Beautiful, and then rise, reborn as Disciples of that Beauty.

Then the two priests bent down, touched the man on the head and shoulders, and fully immersed him three times into the sea, baptizing him "in the name of the Father, and of the Son, and of the Holy Spirit," as commanded by Christ himself (Matthew 28.18). For a few moments the new Christian appeared overwhelmed by emotion. But after clasping his hands together in heartfelt prayer, he carefully waded back to the steps and was met by the two junior monks, who helped him back onto shore. He quickly dried himself off with a towel before receiving Chrismation, the seal of the Holy Spirit, the ultimate fulfillment of the baptismal rite.

In receiving the oil of holy Chrism—applied to the face, hands, heart, and feet—Christians, through grace, become like living temples dedicated to God. They transform into potential channels of divine energy and begin the spiritual path of *theosis* that leads to deification. In short, they invisibly become like Christ in the world, anointed Spirit-bearers of Truth; by degrees they take on the image of the Everlasting in whom they have been consecrated. And like Christ, they mystically become ministers of creation, sanctified links between heaven and earth, empowered overseers of a world desperately in need of loving order and direction.

In receiving Chrismation, all these attributes and gifts are sealed within the baptized. The Holy Spirit enters into the depths of the heart "with sighs too deep for words" (Romans 8.26), and there dwells eternally, no matter how careless and indifferent the convert may become. Thus as the elder priest anointed the newborn Christian, the entire congregation sang the very old and stirring hymn "All who have been baptized in the Lord have put on Christ forevermore."

After a brief tonsuring (symbolic of sacrifice in the Orthodox baptismal rite), the confirmed believer was then led by the clergy back to the monastery where, in the courtyard chapel, he would receive his first Holy Communion. As the gathered assembly slowly filed into the abbey, I considered how this "palace by the sea" represented the divine kingdom, both spiritually and aesthetically. And in a very real way, the newly anointed servant of the Lord was about to receive his King, in the form of the body and blood of Christ, the last step in a series of sacraments meant to intimately prepare the convert for the new life in God.

When I arrived at the chapel, I found that the space within the small church had already filled, so I took a seat along the perimeter of the courtyard. There, cooled by a welcome breeze,

I meditated on the great and awesome mystery I had just witnessed.

A man had been joined to the living body of Christ and his holy Church. A believer had, for all time and unto eternity, been mystically engrafted into the community of God, entering into a sanctified relationship with Jesus (and with all believers) since the time of the resurrection. He now had a more refined and conscious access to the Creator, the Christ "through whom all things were made" (John 1.3).

Via prayer and good deeds, the newly baptized could exercise a powerful intercessory role in the stability and harmony of the cosmos. He had been figuratively transformed into a minister and overseer of creation, an emissary of peace and light who could more readily draw upon Agape, the loving power with which he had been invested, for the healing of both self and society. He had entered into the "Priesthood of the Laity" (1 Peter 2.4-10, 3.21-22), into which every baptized Christian is called in order to help elevate, purify, sanctify and bless everything in the cosmos. Henceforth he would be living in two realms, the heavenly and the earthly, acting as a theocentric bridge between both, that communion between humanity and God might be increasingly restored. Through grace, he now possessed the remarkable gift of helping to usher in the kingdom of the Lord, the bright joy of life and light that will illuminate the universe on the last day.

Through a narrow window cut into a wall of the monastery, I could just make out the sea below, streaming out to the sunlit horizon. As I watched the waves ripple gently, it occurred to me that the rainbow arcs I had seen "moving over the face of the waters" most accurately represented the hope that baptized

Christians radiate and extend to others as they journey toward
the God of eternity.

This hope is the miracle of baptism. It opens the mystic door
through which the believer and Christ may communicate vis-
ibly and invisibly, in ways both seen and unforeseen. The gates
of heaven open, that love's blessings may flow freely, brilliantly,
and without end.

> The Water that I shall give will become,
> in those who partake of it, a Fountain
> springing up unto Everlasting Life.
>
> (John 4.14)

Seaside monastery, Patmos, Greece.

S.T. GEORGIOU, 1995.

Glimpsing Shangri-La

Towards the end of my graduate program, I received word from a friend in Ireland, Fr. Tom, that two Tibetan lamas (monks) had been visiting Dublin and would be coming to Berkeley as part of their world peace pilgrimage. Fr. Tom had introduced the monks to the life and writings of Thomas Merton, and then went on to show them *The Way of the Dreamcatcher*, my book on Robert Lax. Though they spoke little English, they were intrigued by the photos of Lax interspersed through the pages, and told Fr. Tom that they would look me up when they came to Berkeley.

Sure enough, I received a call from one of the monks some time later. They were in town and wished to arrange a meeting.

It was agreed that at 5 p.m. I would pick them up at Shattuck and Durant, a downtown intersection, since they had planned to sightsee in the area during the afternoon. We would then drive to a friend's house for a small dinner party.

Strange as it may seem, it had not occurred to me how I would recognize the monks! Only when I was heading down Shattuck did this thought cross my mind. I must have taken it for granted that they would be wearing their robes, and so would be easy to spot in the crowds.

Thankfully, this was the case. There they were, an older lama and what looked like his younger disciple, standing on a corner, fully decked out in their crimson-maroon regalia. They might as well have dropped out of the sky from Lhasa! Radiant and serene in the downtown bustle, they were attracting the attention of passersby, a number of whom put their hands together in a reverent gesture of greeting, which the monks straightaway returned.

I pulled up and waved. With big smiles, they walked over to my neon-blue Honda and half-bowed, saying, "Happy colour!" (Blue is a favourite colour of Tibetans, as it represents wisdom, purity and faith; the colour is also associated with limitless spiritual energy, boundless as the sky.)

Before I had a chance to thank them for the compliment, they broke into a brief chant, then explained that they had just blessed my car. When I told them that it had also been blessed by a Greek Orthodox priest, they nodded vigorously, saying, "More power! All blessings good!"

In this joyous interfaith spirit we drove to the dinner party. Not much was said along the way, though we kept on smiling. The older monk waved his hands around as he took in the sights. His younger disciple, who spoke better English, read various street signs aloud and seemed to grasp their meaning.

It was a powerful experience sitting next to the lamas, riding with these spiritual men from a faraway land. I never would have met them had it not been for my work with Robert Lax. In opening his door to me on Patmos, it seemed that other doors of enlightenment had been opening ever since.

When we arrived at my friend's house, we were ushered into the living room and began to eat an assortment of appetizers. Many of the spicy-vegetarian dishes were new to the lamas, who relished them. They asked to sit on the floor, so we all sat down cross-legged, a position that was most favoured, coincidentally, by Lax. As Merton had remarked in *The Seven Storey Mountain*, "Lax talked best sitting on the floor."[83]

In the course of our conversation, I learned that the two monks belonged to the Karma Kargyud sect, one of the four main schools of Tibetan Buddhism. They were especially devoted to the saint and poet Milarepa (1040–1123), whose illustrious pupil, Gampopa, founded the Kargyud school. The older monk was, in fact, a *Rinpoche*, meaning a "Great Precious One," an incarnate lama of high rank, and his younger disciple had been his pupil for fifteen years. Born and raised in Tibet, the monks eventually entered a large monastery in Dharamsala, India, the "residence in exile" of the Dalai Lama since the Chinese Communist invasion of Tibet in 1959.

As we continued with dinner and then took our dessert, I spoke about the interfaith activity of Merton, and then gifted the monks with my book on Lax. When they heard Merton's name, they put their hands together as if to pray and said, "In Ireland, Fr. Tom told us about this Christian man—so good, loving, big-hearted."

Then they opened up my book and, grinning broadly, pointed to Lax. The Rinpoche kept running his finger over Lax's photo, intermittently pointing to me. Then he motioned to his young apprentice and finally to himself, indicating that the four of us had a teacher-student relationship in common. Leaning towards me, he brought the book close to his heart and said, very slowly, "Teachers and books open mind; we learn peace that way. Keep writing things like this."

Everything began to feel increasingly blessed. I was sharing a fellowship meal not only with monks from another religion and culture, but with men of faith who appreciated my work and spiritual journey, and I, theirs. We were not trying to convert one another, but were respectfully learning from each other's traditions, beliefs and personal history. Like Lax and Brahmachari (a Hindu ascetic whom Lax had befriended in college),[84] the lamas and I understood that we were already living and growing in the presence of the Holy, each of us in our own way, according to the precious and ancient faith systems into which we were born. What remained was to sincerely acknowledge and honour our respective paths, and to "maintain the unity of the Spirit in the bond of peace" (Ephesians 4.3).

As the dinner came to a close, the Rinpoche laughed aloud and said something to me that I did not understand, though I heard him use the word "reincarnation." Then the Tibetan elder asked his disciple to make clear what he was trying to communicate.

"Rinpoche says he knew you in a past life—you were lamas together!" said the young man happily.

"That's astounding," I replied, looking into the elder's joyful eyes. "But how does he know?"

"It is something Rinpoche feels," replied the disciple. "He just knows."

I nodded my head, taking the elder's exuberant pronouncement as an expression of friendship and affection. Though as an Orthodox Christian I did not believe in reincarnation, I felt honoured that he had thought of me in this deeply interconnected and spiritual way.

I tried to convey these thoughts to the Rinpoche, but whether or not he understood, he didn't say. He just kept on smiling, and when I dropped the monks off at their residence, he told me that we would meet again.

"In this life or the next?" I joked, knowing that they had only a short stay in Berkeley.

The monks simply bowed and bade me goodbye.

A week later, as I was having lunch with my friend David at an outdoor café on Berkeley's College Avenue, our subject of conversation turned to the Tibetan monks. I was describing to him the joy I felt in meeting them, when who should suddenly glide by but the lamas themselves! The timing could not have been more perfect, and for a second or two I wasn't sure if I was awake or caught up in a dream. I called out to them, and when they saw us we all burst out laughing.

The Rinpoche put his hands together and bowed, saying to me, "Such happy, happy feelings! Last week, reincarnation; today, Nirvana!"

Arrowblessing

The day before my dissertation defense—the last hurdle in earning the Ph.D.—I decided to take a long walk by the sea to mentally prepare myself for the upcoming three-hour ordeal. Soon I would be in the examination room, facing a committee intent on asking deep and incisive questions regarding a lengthy work that had taken me years to complete.

Though I was well familiar with the topic (the spiritual elements inherent in the thought and poetry of Robert Lax), my mind kept going blank when I imagined myself seated before the faculty the next morning. It was strange that I had spent the last ten years learning about Lax (and, for seven of those years, had intermit- tently met with him), and yet now, at the culminating point of my academic program, I felt so empty-headed, as if I knew only the most minimal things pertaining to his life.

It was not that I had actually forgotten about the poet and his work—far from it. The problem was that while there was so much to say about him, everything concerning the sage pointed to simplicity, peace of mind, meditative quiet, holy stillness, and infinite nothingness. Lax's ascetic spirituality and verse centred on a transcendent God, a mystery who hid himself in a "Cloud of Unknowing." Much waiting and self-emptying were necessary to find this apophatic God, for he revealed himself at his own discretion, and in ways that transcended human expression.

In defending my work, a scholastic study having to do with an austere minimalist who believed that less is spiritually more, I would be using a plethora of words to point to what is ultimately unutterable. Strangely, I had not dwelled on this paradox in writing the dissertation, perhaps because my single-minded drive to delineate the reductionist influences on Lax drove the project to completion. But now, quite suddenly, at this critical juncture, the fact that I was about to defend a 300-page work on a preeminent minimalist who daily exercised "spiritual simplicity" and rigorously practised "economy of form" loomed large.

How could I speak at length on a poet-mystic whose one-word praise songs to the Creator ran like repetitive mantras, page after page? And how could I deliver a substantive defense when considering how much of the dissertation would revolve around the hidden, unknowable God on whom Lax had so often waited in empty silence?

To calm my nerves, I took a drive out to the beach and walked down the windy coast. While looking out over the sunny crests, I saw something glimmer in the swells. Long and bright, quite thin, it steadily rolled in with the surf, bobbing irregularly until it was flung on the sand. Rushing toward it, I found that the sea had cast forth a yellow arrow. It had spewed out of the depths like a mystic sign, a portent of direction.

The wave-born bolt seemed to figuratively point to my impending defense. Moreover, it was *yellow*, a primary colour that Lax had greatly favoured. He regularly used it when adding dot designs to postcards and letters he would send me. One of the last things he did before dying was inscribe 30 or so copies of his last publication, *The Peacemaker's Handbook*, with a simple yellow dot on the title page.[85] He had just enough strength left to accomplish this.

And then it dawned on me that, years before, I had once asked Lax if his signature dot had something to do with the *bindu*, a tiny round Hindu symbol designating a cosmic starting point from which anything may emerge and take shape. This dot was the sacred gateway (or interdimensional aperture) pinpointing the link between the unformed and forming universe.

Lax replied that his yellow dots were simply dots, a response characteristic of his self-effacing nature. Yet while I held the new-found arrow, I realized that when an arrowhead pierces through its target, it leaves an enlarged ring, a kind of dot. And since the arrow I grasped was yellow, it almost seemed as if Lax had let it fly from the other shore. I felt as though he had shot it through the void to reassure me that all would go well the next morning.

Since ancient times, the arrow has been considered a powerful spiritual symbol, particularly in Zen Buddhism, a faith familiar to Lax. The weapon represents a kind of penetrative awareness, a piercing of illusion, anxiety, and doubt to get to the heart of the matter.

In finding this feathered shaft by the sea, I felt that Lax was ultimately telling me that soon I would be releasing my own arrow—the last bolt of my doctoral program. To hit the mark, all I needed to do was let go of my uncertainty and place my trust in the mystery of grace that had guided me to Patmos (and to Lax) in the first place. The arrow would find the target on its own, just as the arrow I held had found me. Or, as the early Taoist Chuang Tzu put it,

> When an archer is shooting for nothing
> He has all his skill.
> If he shoots for a brass buckle
> He is already nervous.
> If he shoots for a prize of gold
> He goes blind or sees two targets—
> He is out of his mind!
>
> And yet his skill has not changed;
> The prize divides him.
> He cares.
> He thinks more of winning
> Than of shooting.
> And the need to win
> Drains him of power.[86]

The following day—with the yellow arrow concealed in my satchel—I went on to give my defense and earned a Ph.D. in Religion and Art. Like the illuminating bolt Lax may have directed my way, I had at last pierced the ultimate.

Food for Thought

At my graduation reception, one of the gifts I received was a black canvas travel bag, large enough to contain lecture notes, books, and slides, items that I regularly use in teaching. It came at the right time, because my other "journeyman's bag" was quite worn after 10 years of use.

After I had emptied the old bag and was about to place it in the trash, I paused to think of all the classrooms and amphitheatres I had carried it into. And I thought of the many things the bag had contained over the years—particularly food. For years I began my classes not with a customary review (or a survey of the impending lecture), but by handing out cans of soup, tuna, beans, bread, cereal, and boxes of crackers and cookies. Especially during the first week of class, this radical practice would puzzle students who, quite naturally, would ask me why I was giving out food. With a smile, I would reply, "Because college students are always hungry!"

Some would be satisfied with this response, but others prodded further. "No other professor gives us food—why do you? Is it a religious thing? Are you trying to earn karmic points?"

Eventually, I would tell them that after a good deal of teaching, I had found a direct relationship between eating and thinking. In life we consume both food for the body and food for the mind. We are what we eat, just as we are what we think. And when eating and thinking come together in a balanced way, both can become tasty, even satiating experiences.

Without a regular supply of food (particularly wholesome food), we cannot think well; and without good thoughts at the table (especially when saying grace), the consumption of food can become a mechanical, even dull exercise. Eating in this fashion may lead to a gradual disinterest in one's diet. Hence the Greeks maintained that a healthy, fortified body helps to fuel a healthy mind, and a vigorous, active mind helps to maintain a sound body.

And yet the link between eating and thinking goes deeper. Phrases like "chew the fat," "chew the cud," and "food for thought" commonly refer to the cognitive process, as does "ruminate," which comes from a Latin word meaning "to chew" or "to reflect and ponder on." When seen in this light, digestion itself (how the body absorbs nutrients from food) and intellection (the mind's absorption of thought) appear to be closely related functions.

Interestingly, the things we eat are also used in the learning process, particularly in the documentation of ideas, and have been for thousands of years. We eat parts of trees and plants;

these organic sources likewise give us paper. We eat fruits, vegetables, and various mineral substances; these same items have been commonly used to create inks, paints, and dyes. Eating and learning thus are holistic processes closely connected with nature.

Especially in old world societies, students met with their teachers outdoors and went on meditative walks. In essence, the environment—the very place where foodstuffs and writing materials originate—was understood as being the sourcepoint of inspiration and learning. Take away the environment, and eating, thinking, and eco-based living could not go on. The foods and thoughts gathered (or generated) through the working of nature were ultimately used to *sustain nature*. The good life centred on delicately making use of the God-given earth, the fruits of which were cyclically offered to the Creator in thanks and in blessing. Wisdom was consequently seen as an organic and theocentric round, wherein all of human effort replenished and did not exploit the ecosystem. Surely this is something we must take heed of today, given the rapidly deteriorating state of the environment.[87]

I also told my students that the reason I gave them food was to teach them patience, an important asset in a dangerously impulsive world. Not everyone received the handouts; I usually had enough for only three or four people per session. But by the end of the semester, the entire class was "fed." All the students had to do was keep on showing up and they would receive their due.

Certainly a parallel may be drawn here with life in God. Most of our lives are spent waiting on the Lord patiently, and with hope.

As long as we continue to do this sincerely and consistently, we shall not go away unfilled. So, in a sense, life in the Spirit is like coming to class—all we have to do is keep on showing up, and eventually, body and soul will be provided with sustenance.

Receiving food in class also taught my students attention. When I instructed in the amphitheatre, sometimes facing nearly 200 people, I might fling small packets of cereal into the audience in a kind of sudden, Zen-like fashion. Those who were alert grabbed the food as it sailed into the seats, whereas the inattentive sadly missed their opportunity.

So much in life has to do with timing and how we direct our consciousness in the moment at hand. Of the many things God calls us to be, we are most called to be attentive to everything around us, to the whole of creation. As stewards of the cosmos, it is our holy duty to nurture, pray, and love all of life back to its origin, that we may complete the cycle of Agape, the bright power from which the universe was born. Only the attentive can hear "the elements groaning, eagerly awaiting the transfiguration of the universe and the revealing of the Children of God" (Romans 8.22-23).

A wealth of knowledge may be found in meditating on the relationship between food and thought—even the limits of both. For while our stomachs can be full, sometimes we still feel hungry and restless. And though from time to time we may experience deep intellectual reverie, our thoughts can quickly turn to anxiety, if not boredom.

Unstable and unable to find lasting satisfaction, we perceive that the pleasures of the senses and the life of the mind are somehow incomplete. Deep within, we long for something more than our mortality can comprehend, and what this fleeting world can offer. We hunger with all we are for the fullness of God, in whom our souls shall at last find peace. All of theology points to this, as does Christ himself, the supreme sustenance of the cosmos. Aptly referred to in Scripture as the "Bread of Life" and the "Eternal Word," he is meant to be mystically consumed by his faithful, wholly absorbed by body, mind, and spirit. Thus when he asks his disciples, shortly after the resurrection, "Do you have anything here to eat?" (Luke 24.41), Jesus figuratively refers to his lifesaving body and blood, the cup of everlasting love and light.

Human salvation was accomplished through God giving himself up for the life and illumination of the world; the entire universe is called to share in his mystic feast. "Education," from a Latin word meaning to "bring forth" and to "bear fruit," also has to do with "feeding the multitudes," as both knowledge and wisdom help to deliver people from the perils of ignorance.

In the complex journey of life, or in the long walk down "Mystic Street," the secret to a calm and fulfilling trek may consequently centre on reaching into one's travel bag, finding whatever food is there, and sharing it with others along the way.

At the Graduate Theological Union, the following words, engraved on a metal plaque, appear over the Pacific School of Religion. They too offer food for thought:

Enter.
Seek.
Find.
Go Forth to Give.

Treasure Chest

A few days after graduation, I was sitting at my desk, idly looking around the room, studying the photographs, posters, and artwork I had acquired while working on the seven-year doctorate. My study looked a bit like the interior of a ship making its way through the Aegean, as there were numerous nautical artifacts on the walls and much memorabilia from Patmos.

As I was taking in the various items, each with its own unique history, my eyes rested on a small ornate container atop a bookcase, half hidden amid papers and accumulated postcards. Made of wood and metal, it was crafted to resemble a treasure chest. I had seen it regularly over the years, to the point where I no longer contemplated its personal significance, but now, all at once, memories of the chest came back to me.

When I was about 16 years old, I had a strong desire to become a physician. I had read numerous books having to do with the human body and compiled a sketchbook of anatomy. A few family members who worked in the health field encouraged me to realize my interests, gifting me with medical encyclopedias and texts on the history of medicine. Through their help, I also later volunteered at a hospital for a short time where I learned first-hand about the profession.

One day, after returning home from the hospital, I found that a package had come for me in the mail. It was the chest; I had won it as a prize in a local poetry contest, the theme of which was travel and adventure. And because the ornate container symbolically represented journeying, I made a spontaneous vow that I would never again open it until I became a physician, at that point my professional destination.

But what to put in the chest prior to locking it? I remember going to my bureau and taking from the tabletop three things that held great significance for me—a copy of the Bible, a tiny fragment from the Parthenon (which my grandmother had brought from Greece as an immigrant), and a golden lapel pin fashioned in the form of the caduceus, the symbol of the medical profession. These I carefully placed in the chest, and after whispering a prayer, shut the lid and bolted the lock.

Of course, I never became a physician. Over the years, my career interests evolved in other directions. I considered dentistry, then law, then journalism, until I finally settled on teaching the Humanities. In the meantime I held various jobs, travelled widely, and worked on various writing projects. Eventually I met Robert Lax, and my academic interests shifted to theology and art, resulting in a doctoral degree in the field.

All the while, the chest had remained sealed. As I ran my hands around its ribbed exterior, fingering its antique padlock, it suddenly came to me that I was now, at last, a "doctor." I was not a physician, but a doctor of philosophy. The attainment of my Ph.D. gave me reason to think that I could finally open the treasure chest.

It was strange and exciting to cradle it and recollect its personal meaning. I felt I was holding a part of time that had stood still, sealed with a vow. I was a boy when I had last closed the lid, and now, 30 years later, I would open it as a man.

What would I feel on opening a chest in which lay the unrealized medical aspirations of my youth? And yet, my doctorate in theology did, in some way, relate to healing, as it dealt with the harmony of the soul. In this little chest my formative, idealistic past was condensed. Would it have any impact on my present and future?

The image of a locked chest, a treasure chest, had great symbolic meaning. Mallarmé, the famous French poet of the nineteenth century, wrote on the subject:

> Every man has a secret in him, many die without finding it, and will never find it because they are dead, it no longer exists, nor do they. I am dead and risen again with the jeweled key of my last spiritual casket. It is up to me now to open it in the absence of any borrowed impression, and its mystery will emanate in a sky of great beauty.[88]

Knowing that opening the chest would be an act of ritual, I decided to take it to the quiet seclusion of Ocean Beach near Fort Funston, a recreation area overlooking the Pacific. There, by the waterside, I popped open the thin metallic lock and lifted up the lid.

I was amazed at how perfectly the Bible fit within the tight rectangular space; the red silk sides of the container were perfectly flush with the holy book. Atop its black leather cover the white stone from the Parthenon and golden caduceus glistened in the light.

In a curious way I felt reborn, handling things I last touched as a youth. This feeling of rejuvenation was profound and intimate, for the contents of the chest directly related to God (the Bible), my ancestral roots (the ancient Greek stone), and healing (the caduceus). Together, the uncovered items symbolized a unity of spirit and body, the divine and human, the invisible and visible. At the same time, they represented the very doctoral degree I had just received—*Religion and Art*—as the Bible, the Parthenon, and the caduceus were deeply spiritual as well as artistic creations meant to harmonically reconnect people with the Origin of All.

Carefully I lifted the Bible out of the chest. I remembered Lax telling me that every so often he would open the Holy Book three times and at random place his finger on a passage, a practice that gave him a sense of spiritual direction. Especially if he were troubled or was unsure about which path to follow, the passages, taken together, helped him to get reoriented—they showed him the way.

I decided to do the same. This was the copy of the Bible that I had read when young; perhaps it was in my hands again for a reason. So I opened it and first turned to St. Paul's defense before the Roman governor Felix.

> Felix sent for Paul and heard him concerning the faith in
> Christ. And while listening to him speak of righteousness,
> self-control, and the judgment to come, Felix became
> afraid. (Acts 24:24-25)

It was a perturbing passage, a sobering wake-up call. Was I
neglecting to live a sound life in God and fearful of the consequences? After thinking about it for a while, I reasoned that my
next selection might clarify the first.

> "Most assuredly, I say to you, the hour is coming, and now
> is, when the dead will hear the voice of the Son of God,
> and those who hear will live!" (John 5.25)

I felt a growing immediacy, a sense of direct (if not dire) urgency,
as if the Second Coming were indeed imminent, and that I
should spiritually prepare myself for it. The admonition seemed
strongly personal, and this was confirmed in the final passage
that I turned to. For when I opened up the Bible the last time,
I came to my own name.

> And the saying pleased the multitude. And they chose
> Stephen, a man full of faith and the Holy Spirit.... (Acts
> 6.5)

I returned the Bible to its chest and looked out over the waves.
From the three passages, it appeared as though I were being
strongly encouraged to discipline and purify myself. Moreover,
it seemed like I was being called. I had just opened up a treasure
chest whose spiritual and artistic contents hearkened to my doctoral program, and then turned to three interrelated selections of
the New Testament that ultimately pointed to my summons.

But a call to what? I was happy where I was, teaching at local colleges and looking forward to an eventual tenured position. My newly earned doctorate would certainly assist me in this endeavour. What else was there left to do?

And then the words of Lax came back to mind, words he had told me a few years after I met him. By that time he knew how much I valued his advice, and how I thought of him as a mentor. And since he had known me for a while, I asked him one night, quite open-heartedly, "What do you think I should do with my life?"

His eyes looked deeply into mine, and in a calm, measured tone, the old poet said, "I think you should be a *papah*, a priest, and find a good girl you can share your life and ministry with."

It was not an answer I was prepared for, nor one that immediately inspired me. I thought of Peter when Christ told him, "Truly, truly, I say to you, when you were young, you girded yourself and walked where you would, but when you are old, another will gird you and carry you where you do not wish to go" (John 21.18). So I did not raise the question again, nor did I reveal this particular exchange to anyone. But in subsequent meetings Lax would periodically hint of his suggestion, sometimes asking me questions about the biblical priest Melchizedek, whose holy order is fulfilled in Christ, an order to which all priests mystically belong.[89] Even the last time I met with the poet, he searchingly asked me, "Who is Melchizedek?"

Strangely enough, I did not sense a need to become a priest. In some ways, I already saw myself acting a bit like one, particularly in my regular attempts to commune with the sanctity of nature and disseminate that holiness. Almost daily I walked by the sea and prayed for the life and health of all things, repeatedly saying a well-known Orthodox supplication, "Holy God, Holy Mighty, Holy Immortal, have mercy upon us." I also made it a point to say often the Jesus Prayer ("Jesus Christ, Son of God, have mercy on me"), and tried to pray for everyone I encountered, be they students, friends, passersby, even animals.

Periodically, I brought holy water to the ocean, especially on Epiphany (for Orthodox Christians, the feast day commemorating Jesus' Baptism, and for all Christians, the manifestation of the Incarnate Word), and would pour it into the sea to bless all marine life, as well as those who worked or played along the shore and who might have perished there. I also made icons from materials I found at the beach, images meant to promote peace in an angry, restless world, and regularly sent shells, sand dollars and stones to the elderly and housebound in the hope that an organic contact with nature might uplift and inspire them. In essence, I was making good the power of my baptism, a divine energy through which I had been figuratively transformed into a "priestly overseer of creation."[90] Like a new Adam, I could access the love and light I had been anointed with for the good of the earth and human community.

And yet despite this natural ministry, I had, at varying times, experienced deeper stirrings with regard to honouring God and the divine creation. Indeed, there were moments when I felt that I could serve him in a more consecrated, sacramental way.

One summer morning on Patmos, as I was passing by a chapel, I saw a young priest within, scrubbing down the white marble altar. Something about this rare sight intensely moved me, and

I stood there by the doorway watching him. With his long dark hair falling about his shoulders and his narrow, angular beard, he resembled Jesus. When he looked up and our eyes met, I sensed him saying, "Why are you standing there? Why don't you help? There is much work to be done." But abruptly I walked on, feeling a faint tinge of remorse.

Some years later, while on a trip to Bodega Bay in California, I was running along a deserted beach in the early morning when I came upon a natural altar made of a raised block of stone, nearly jet black. The fissured rock stood right at the shoreline where the waves broke on the sand. Laying my hands on the massive ebony slab, I started saying prayers there, beneath the beauty of the open sky.

Looking out over the sea, I suddenly felt a visceral longing to conduct the Divine Liturgy, if only as a thank offering to God. In that fleeting moment I yearned to become an ordained channel through which God's holy mystery might be imparted. And then it came to me that I had sometimes felt this desire, however faint and ephemeral, when teaching college classes in religion. But now the urge to say Mass seemed very intense and compelling. "The call" had become increasingly tangible and real.

All at once, becoming a minister seemed the obvious, most natural thing to do. What better way to offer my gratitude to the Creator and creation than by becoming a priest? Why not follow the example of Jesus and give up my life (or, more realistically, enhance it) for the welfare of the cosmos? Had I not already experienced moments of transcendence, in which I felt God near? Was I not already halfway through my existence? What greater work was I waiting for? Salvation had come, the Good

News was here and now. Perhaps the universal cycles kept going on because sensitive souls all over the planet had elected to give their entire selves to God. Perhaps birds flew, the sun rose and set, and the earth spun because a pure and steadfast love for the Lord of Love emanated from people of faith the world over, transforming ardent believers into ministers of Agape.

And yet through grace I was an artist and teacher, and in this dual manner could continue to serve God well. Was it necessary that after years of schooling, I enter the seminary? Then again, the very word "seminary" implies *seed*, a kind of becoming. This strong link to nature attracted me. A seed encapsulates growth, potential, and demonstrates a simple beauty; by merely resting in the earth it gently flowers and enhances the universe, in turn creating more seeds and flowers. In a similar way, we too were meant to rest in God, to "grow and flow with him," as Lax liked to put it.

The religious philosopher Simone Weil said that all of our hungering for nature, for beauty, and for a loving companion with whom we can celebrate life, all of the inborn longing that we experience in our brief existence is ultimately a yearning for the Incarnated Christ—the great Mystery for which everything was created.[91] All things were made through him, we live in him now, and we were created to rejoice in him forever; therefore apart from him, there can be no greater love. Whether we know it at this point or not, everything is a journey toward this ultimate realization.

In my own spiritual odyssey, I had gradually reached this point of understanding, and was now at a crossroads. It was a difficult time, wondering which way to go: to continue being a university professor and artist, or redirect my energies and serve God in a more concentrated and ordained fashion. My heart needed to devote itself to what was most necessary and beneficial, a way of growth and fruition good for both myself and the cosmos. Certainly the earth needed more intercessory activity—from all walks of life—to survive.

I had arrived at a place of burning, the junction of zero where nonessentials had to be eliminated so I could clearly see the road ahead. To some degree, this was already happening, for when I wasn't teaching, I was spending much of my time trekking up and down the shore at Land's End, thinking about what was the most important thing to do.

I still walk out there. At the edge of the sea I can better listen to my thoughts; things are getting clearer, more refined. A kind of *kenosis*, or self-emptying continues in my life, that I may discover the inmost intentions of my heart and become certain of my path.

Oftentimes along the shore, I deeply sense how the primacy of love makes all things in the universe seem insignificant in comparison, because ultimately, Agape is all there really is. Love is why we are here, why we even *are*, and everything in our midst is meant to teach us this holy truth. Our principal goal in life should therefore be to acquire the Spirit of that Love and disseminate it joyously, unreservedly, like the loving, giving God in whose living waters we flow. Whatever path we take, whatever pursuits we may ultimately accomplish, as long as we do our work with an open, loving heart, we will have made good our divine birthright; we will have become everything we were meant to be.

As I watch the waves and contemplate my future in Christ—a future still uncertain, lived day by day in faith—a poem that I had recently written to my friend Vito, the Italian artist whom I met on Patmos, keeps coming to mind. It speaks of an inner poverty that is spiritually awakening, liberating, and blessed. It is the place (and locus of grace) where I now am, and where many other searchers may be, somewhere along "Mystic Street."

> Yes, I would like my own house,
> but maybe the universe is my house.
> I am the crazy man on the beach
> singing in the moonlight,
> poor, naked, and free.
> My dear brother, we know
> what the earth tastes like.
> We cut our bread on the stars
> and drink the morning sun.
> Our way has been long
> and winding, and that
> is the beauty of it,
> long and winding
> like a distant wave,
> like a desert trail,
> or a tree slowly
> growing,
> twisting
> into
> the
> sky.

S.T. GEORGIOU, 2005.

We remain "works in transit," riding the spiritual railway that leads further and further into the heart of God. In this increasingly luminous and loving expanse there is no end, only infinitely happy beginnings.

Epilogue

As I walk along the beach, looking for stones and shell fragments useful in my icon work, I am steadily seeing how many of the experiences described in this book have to do with finding spiritual meaning not only in everyday situations, but also in the "alley of the insignificant"—in what much of society may deem marginal, inconsequential and valueless. Hence my continued use of castaway items in art, solitary treks along Land's End, and deep appreciation of the rustic life—all of which help to generate a pure and simple relationship with God, and promote a more intuitive self-understanding of unconditional love and grace.

In completing my theological studies (and in my progressive attempts to live simply and compassionately), I had made empathetic connections not only with students and professors, but also with campus workers, sidewalk strangers, subway riders, priests, monks, artists, and Patmos islanders. Occasionally, the poor, homeless, and more marginal elements of society came into my life, sometimes entirely on their own, such as when the three shabbily dressed toughs suddenly gifted me with an icon card of Mary of Medjugorje, and when the barefoot boy in ragged clothing walked by my house reciting from Revelation. Even in my teaching, students on the edge (near failing) would follow me about after class, wishing to talk at length about spiritual issues. Their presence reminded me that while they were not making the grade, they were still showing up to class, and perhaps in the long run, that in itself was enough.

When I wasn't studying or teaching, I found myself heading for distant places, such as Patmos and the California wilds, in which I prayed and meditated, communing with creation and Creator. In these solitary locales I quietly listened to the "Other Power" perpetually giving Life to the world. The Life given issued inexhaustibly, without reserve, as exemplified by the cross with the missing centre I had found at Ocean Beach; in giving up his Son, God became "poor and empty" for the renewal of the cosmos. And yet in doing so, the divine Giver inversely became infinitely full. Consubstantially empty and full, he eternally remains the mysterious bright void out of which life once emanated and shall ultimately return. Even now, by unique and ascendant degrees, creation is intimately fusing with the Love that brought everything into being out of its all-holy charity and inconceivable nothingness.

Many of my friends also sought out the deity in nature, and in remote, ascetic places. Gianvito Lo Greco heard God's voice in the desert, near Masada. He, too, understood that the Lord inexhaustibly sustains the earth; out of the barren wasteland God whispered to him, in the wind, *I Am*.

Both of us received our spiritual and creative inspiration through Robert Lax, the hermit and minimalist poet who radiated spiritual simplicity in his life and thought. His very being demonstrated that in order to "go with the Flow," it is best to travel light—hence the wisdom of emptying oneself of all things superfluous in order to live an authentic and theocentric life.

In doing so, one no longer remains mesmerized by current trends and the latest breaking news, but lives on a deeper level, tapping into the more constant Current coursing through the cosmos, the love of God holding all things together—the "one thing needful" (Luke 10.42), however perilous the times.

It is both in and through this love that we are made free, that we learn to realize our place in the world. And it is by trusting in its mystery and grace that our lives are made complete, because we place our faith in the power that conceived us long before our birth, and in which we "live, move, and have our being," both now and forever.

As for my own journey, I can only say that in love, I can confidently go on to the next stage, whatever that may be. Like everyone gifted with life, I remain a work in transit, riding the spiritual railway that leads further and further into the Heart of God, in which there is no end, only infinitely happy beginnings.

The poet Theodore Roethke said, "I learn by going where I have to go." One may also say, "I learn by *loving* where I have to go." Certainly my experiences en route to the Ph.D. in theology have taught me this. Indeed, perhaps the greatest education I received was not cultivated in the classroom, but on "Mystic Street." And yet the spiritual foundation provided by my doctoral studies significantly helped to make these experiences possible, and for this I shall always be grateful.

It has been said that all of our comings and goings in life, all of our prolonged and momentary wanderings, constitute our greater journey in God. If we could somehow retrace them, a beautiful pattern would steadily emerge, much like a sand dollar's imprint, or the crystalline matrix of a snowflake. Perhaps this is because we are already living in an infinitely exquisite Matrix, which, outside of our finite realm of knowing, is nurturing us, praying its life into us as we live and love from day to day.

We exist in a tri-fold energy field: that of Genesis, the Incarnation, and the Resurrection. There can be no greater power for us in this transient cosmos, and that is why we are living on "Mystic Street." Anything is possible as we move toward a new heaven and a new earth, and toward the Second Coming of the Christ who will restore all things to their first-born glory.

In such an increasingly miraculous and changing universe, in a cosmos that for eons has been "groaning for its transfiguration" (Romans 8.22), sometimes we can only exercise patience, despite our eagerness to embrace the God of Love. Like everything in creation, we are called to "wait on Him."[92] For in the eternally dynamic mystery of life, all we can really do is keep trusting our Source and faithfully "go with the Flow," which is precisely what we are doing right now. Perhaps this is why one of the oldest names for Christianity is, quite simply, "The Way" (Acts 19.23; John 14.6).

No point in asking where I go next;
I go wherever you take me.
Go gladly to and gladly from;
I only want to know you're there...

I know that you love me.
I know the things you tell me to do
are from love.

You don't tell me to kill.
You don't tell me to die.
You tell me to love.
You tell me to do the things love does.
You show me the way.

Robert Lax, from *Psalm*[93]

$\mathcal{P}$ostscript

While finishing *Mystic Street*, I received word from Anita, an elderly spiritual friend with whom I kept in touch during my doctoral studies, that she had terminal cancer and only a few months left to live. Before visiting her, I drove out to the seashore to find a special "blessing gift." After I found what I was looking for (or it found me), I placed it in a box along with this note. The message perhaps best explains why this life is a mystic passage, and why we are steadily riding love's holy spiritwaves back to their blessed beginning.

> *HI, ANITA!* Today I found a few things for you at Ocean Beach—half of a seashell and a small fossilized sand dollar (which I have placed within the shell). Sometimes these "treasures" wash off the barrier reef that spans the shore.
>
> The sand dollar is about one and a half million years old, older than us, if we believe that the physical universe was created long before humans were. It's nice holding something that precedes us, giving us continuity to the Origin, and with all things that have issued from the Source.

And the fossil's flowery rays indicate that even a million years can't erase a radiant design, which we are too. Its expansive sunburst has been blessed with seawater from Patmos (which I always keep a vial of), holy water from the Greek Orthodox Church (received on Epiphany), and holy water from Lourdes. I hope the sand dollar shall work as a powerful instrument of meditation and will infuse you with lots of positive, transformative energy.

Now as for the seashell, where its *other half* is, I haven't a clue. Perhaps the missing piece is a sign that while we're here, all of us are like "half-shells"; we become whole when the waves cast us onto the Other Shore.

In Christian iconography, a shell symbolizes *pilgrimage*. Indeed, we are born pilgrims, and we are all journeying toward the Holiest Site of All, each in our own way and in our own good time. And when both halves of our respective shells come together, we will have found our "Pearl of Great Price" within, the Light-Core from which all things will flower and begin again.

PEACE AND LOVE TO YOU ALONG THE WAY

~~~~~MEGA-BLESSINGS~~~~~

~~~~AGAPE~~~~

STEVE

There are only two ways to live your life.
One is as though nothing is a miracle.
The other is as though everything is a miracle.

Albert Einstein

Love all the earth, every ray of God's light,
every grain of sand and blade of grass,
every living thing. If you love the earth enough,
you will know the divine mystery.

Fyodor Dostoyevsky

Life is not a problem
to be solved, but a
Mystery to be lived.

Gabriel Marcel

Roads Go Over On.

J.R.R. Tolkien

The cosmos was born in joyful love
and toward joyful love we are heading...
It's "one spaceship" as they say.
I think that we are moving toward
a more unified, loving universe
as we journey to the stars.

Robert Lax

Notes

[1]   A mystic is one who, above all, seeks the knowledge and love of God, and, in the process, becomes increasingly aware of the holy power sustaining existence. Through transformative levels of consciousness, or via instantaneous rapture, the mystic experiences an intuitive and spiritual relationship with the boundless energy of Divine Life. He or she integrates with the Infinite; intense feelings of "Oneness" prevail. Nearly every faith lays claim to a mystical tradition, and there are many different kinds of mystics, all of whom come to access the *Guha*, Sanskrit for "the Cave of the Heart," the place of deepest interiority where we are one with God. On mysticism in general, two fundamental classics are William James's *The Varieties of Religious Experience* and Evelyn Underhill's *Mysticism*. See also *The Foundations of Christian Mysticism*, by Barnard McGinn, and *Mystical Experience and Religious Doctrine: An Investigation of the Study of Mysticism in World Religions*, by Philip Almond. Two recent books serve as good introductions to the subject: Ursula King's *Christian Mystics* and Wayne Teasdale's *The Mystic Heart: Discovering a Universal Spirituality in the World's Religions*.

[2]   Barnes, Jonathan. *Early Greek Philosophy* (New York: Penguin Books, 1987), 179.

[3]   "Orthodox" is a Greek term meaning upright (correct) worship. Like the Roman Catholic Church, the Orthodox (or Eastern Orthodox) Church claims to be the first Christian Church founded by Jesus and disseminated by his twelve apostles. For the first thousand years of Christendom, there was, essentially, simply *one* Church, but in 1054, a disastrous schism ("The Great Schism") occurred between the East and West, primarily over papal authority and infallibility. The result was the formation of the "Orthodox East" and the "Catholic (or Latin) West." While the Eastern Church is administered by the Ecumenical Patriarch of Constantinople, the leader of the Western Church is the Pope of Rome.

Eastern Orthodoxy distinguishes itself from Catholicism through its ancient and unchanging rituals, emphasis on the Holy Mystery of

God, prolific use of icons and incense, heart-centred and mantra-like prayer, and married clergy. For more on the Orthodox Church, see *The Orthodox Way* by Bishop Kallistos Ware (St. Vladimir's Seminary Press, 1993) and *The Spirituality of the Christian East, Volume 2: Prayer*, by Tomas Spidlik. Translated by Anthony Gythiel (Cistercian Publications, 2005).

Since the mid-20th century, repeated and expanded efforts have been made to heal the Great Schism of 1054, that the Churches of the East and West might be entirely reunited. The late Pope John Paul II referred to the Catholic and Orthodox Churches as "the two great lungs of Christendom." It should be recognized that the Christian East and West share a millennium of common tradition. To this day, both churches offer the same sacraments and are governed according to a similar ecclesiastic administration (bishops, priests, deacons). In light of the initial unity of the Eastern and Western Churches and their shared commitment in Christ, it is the hope of many Orthodox and Catholic believers that a complete reconciliation between both Churches might be accomplished before 2054 (this date corresponds to the 1,000-year mark following the Great Schism). Notably, in November 2006, a historic ecumenical service commemorating the visit of Pope Benedict XVI to the Ecumenical Patriarchate of Constantinople was conducted at the Holy Trinity Greek Orthodox Church in San Francisco (see *The San Francisco Chronicle*, November 30, 2006).

For more on Eastern Orthodox and Catholic unity, see *The Quest for Unity: Orthodox and Catholics in Dialogue*, edited by John Borelli and John Erickson (St. Vladimir's Seminary Press, 1996) and *Reclaiming the Great Tradition: Evangelicals, Catholics, and Orthodox in Dialogue*, edited by James Cutsinger (Intervarsity, 1997). See also the *Orientale Lumen Conference* website: www.olconference.com.

[4]   *The Way of the Dreamcatcher: Spirit Lessons with Robert Lax, Poet-Peacemaker-Sage* (Novalis, 2002). The text is a personal tribute to the man Thomas Merton believed "had an inborn direction to the living God" (*The Seven Storey Mountain*, New York: Harcourt Brace, 1948, 181, 237), and of whom the Italian poet Francesco Conz said, "He will be remembered as *the last of the mystics* who closed a former epoch" (*The ABC's of Robert Lax*, London: Stride, 1999, 218). Written in dia-

logue format, *The Way of the Dreamcatcher* gives readers the chance to
visit Lax in his remote hilltop hermitage and learn from the man many
have affectionately termed "a saint." The poet's wisdom and depth of
compassion were noted by a host of authors in the Spring 2001 issue
of *The Merton Seasonal* (Vol. 26, No. 1), a publication devoted entirely
to Lax.

For more on Lax's saintly qualities, see *Merton and Friends*, by Jim
Harford (New York: Continuum, 2006). Herein, Harford describes
how, after Lax gave a poetry reading at the *Jubilee* magazine offices in
New York and was entertaining questions, somebody asked him about
heaven. When Lax replied, "I'm looking forward to the time when I
meet Jesus face to face," a close friend of Lax's, Ed Rice, exclaimed,
"How will anybody tell them apart?" (284). Also in *Merton and Friends*,
(110), Harford aptly discerns how a poem that Lax had written on the
prophet Elias, published in the Franciscan magazine, *The Scapular*, July,
1963, seems more like a portrait of Lax himself:

Nobody knows what makes a man a prophet.
He usually does not want to be one, anyway.
God builds a fire in him, then he begins
to do the things a prophet does
and to be what a prophet is.
He works at every moment
with the Holy Spirit.
He learns to choose.
He watches and listens,
not to every sight
and every sound,
but to the sight
that is a sign,
the sound that is
a whisper of the Lord.

5   S.T. Georgiou, *Sea and Sky: Robert Lax and the Spiritual
Dimensions of Minimalism* (2005). Doctoral thesis, GTU, Berkeley.

6   See *The Way of the Dreamcatcher*, 199. A number of recent books
have been published on coincidental and serendipitous phenomena
and their role in psycho-spiritual growth. These in-depth studies in-

clude: Robert Hocke, *There Are No Accidents* (New York: Riverhead, 1998); Craig Bell, *Comprehending Coincidence: Synchronicity and Personal Transformation* (New York: Chrysalis, 2000); Patricia Upczak, *Synchronicity, Signs, and Symbols* (New York: Synchronicity Publishers, 2001). A well-known study in this field, by C.G. Jung, is *Psychology of Religion and Synchronicity* (New York: SUNY Press, 1990).

7   *Tao Te Ching: The Way and Its Power.* Arthur Waley, trans. (New York: Grove, 1958), 47.

8   Evans-Wentz, *The Tibetan Book of the Great Liberation* (London: Oxford University Press, 1954), 230.

9   For example, see *Confessions*, 1.1: "O God, you have made us for Yourself, and our hearts are restless until they rest in You." Augustine. *The Confessions.* R.S Pine-Coffin, trans. (Middlesex: Penguin Books, 1961).

10   Chrysostom. *On the Incomprehensibility of God.* Sermon 5.

11   *Dialogues with Silence.* Jonathan Montaldo, ed. (San Francisco: Harper-San Francisco, 2001), 13.

12   According to the Mahayana Buddhist tradition, Bodhisattvas are beings who strive for Buddhahood (ultimate personal enlightenment) through virtuous practice and the exercise of compassion. Though they take on saintly attributes and eventually become worthy of Nirvana, they renounce complete entry into the "bliss realms" until all beings are saved. For more on this tradition, see *The Way of the Bodhisattva,* one of the great classics of Mahayana Buddhism, written by the eighth-century Indian monk Shantideva (Boston: Shambhala, 1997). On the comparative aspects of Bodhisattvas and Christian saints, see *The Gethsemani Encounter: A Dialogue on the Spiritual Life by Buddhist and Christian Monastics.* D.W. Mitchell and James Wiseman, O.S.B., eds. (New York: Continuum, 1997), and *Purity of Heart and Contemplation: A Monastic Dialogue Between Christian and Asian Traditions.* Bruno Barnhart and Joseph Wong, eds. (New York: Continuum, 2001).

13   "Vita Nuova," from *Modern Greek Poetry.* Kimon Friar, trans. (Athens: Efstathiades Group, 1982), 81.

14   The Dominican School of Philosophy and Theology at the GTU has since moved to a nearby location, although the appearance of the former building still remains generally similar, even after a recent renovation.

15   *Science*. 1984. April 7; 224 (4647); 420–421.

16   Augustine. *Confessions*. 9.10.

17   Moderate exposure to sunlight has been found beneficial in cases of rickets, tuberculosis, various respiratory ailments, jaundice, acne, psoriasis, and in preventing seasonal affective disorder (SAD), a depressive, mood-altering condition, sometimes referred to as "winter blues."

18   For a good selection of Eastern Orthodox hymns (in the Russian tradition), see *Sacred Treasures: Choral Masterworks from Russia*, available through Hearts of Space (www.hos.com).

19   Due to campus renovation work (2005–2006), this zig-zag pathway (and its surrounding area) has been somewhat modified.

20   *Selections from the Notebooks of Leonardo da Vinci*. I.A. Richter, ed. (London: Oxford University Press, 1959), 288.

21   Increasingly, modern medicine is discovering how paranormal incidents involving "expanding consciousness" (events that cannot be explained rationally and that transcend the physical senses) are, in fact, quite common and universal. Voices of reassurance are heard by believers, agnostics, and atheists from all walks of life. Guiding or helpful voices are often heard by those who are close to peril or who have recently lost a loved one. Dr. Larry Dossey, the well-known physician and author of nine books on the role of spirituality in healing, including *Healing Words: The Power of Prayer*, devoted an entire chapter of his latest book to the phenomenon of hearing voices. See *The Extraordinary Power of Ordinary Things* (New York: Harmony, 2006), 209–228.

22   These icons are the work of Robert J. Andrews, one of the premier specialists in Byzantine-style mosaic iconography in America. For the last 40 years, he has designed and installed the extensive mosaics in

Holy Trinity Greek Orthodox Church in San Francisco. In 2007, the capstone to this great project will be completed—the portrait of Christ to be set in the 3,400-square-foot interior dome. The mosaic face of Jesus will be the largest of its kind in the Western hemisphere.

23   For more on theosis (also termed "divinization"), see Vladimir Lossky, *The Mystical Theology of the Eastern Church* (New York: St. Vladimir's Seminary Press, 1976). See also Olivier Clement, *The Roots of Christian Mysticism* (New York: New City Press, 1995), and George Maloney, S.J., *A Theology of Uncreated Energies* (Milwaukee, WI: Marquette University Press, 1978).

24   This is a traditional Kenyan blessing.

25   *The Selected Writings of Gertrude Stein* (New York: Vintage, 1990).

26   From a letter by Tolstoy to his son. *Wise Thoughts for Every Day: On God, Love, Spirit, and Living a Good Life.* Leo Tolstoy. Peter Serikin, trans. (New York: Arcade, 2005).

27   On Father Arrupe, see *Pedro Arrupe, S.J. Essential Writings.* Kevin Burke, ed. (New York: Orbis, 2004).

28   Athanasius. *On the Incarnation* (New York: St. Vladimir's Seminary Press, 1975).

29   *The ABC's of Robert Lax.* David Miller and Nicholas Zurbrugg, eds. (London: Stride, 1999), 89.

30   Bergson. *Introduction to Metaphysics* (New York: Hackett Publishing, 1999), 27–28.

31   Isak Dinesen. *Seven Gothic Tales* (New York: Vintage, 1991).

32   Another version of the Jesus Prayer is "Lord Jesus Christ, Son of God, have mercy upon me, a sinner." For more on the Jesus Prayer (which is essentially derived from Luke 18.13) see *The Jesus Prayer* by Archimandrite Lev Gillet (New York: St. Vladimir's Seminary Press, 1987); *The Art of Prayer.* Timothy Ware, ed. (New York: Faber and Faber, 1966) and *Living the Jesus Prayer,* by Irma Zaleski (Ottawa: Novalis, 1997).

33   *The Ladder of Divine Ascent.* Colm Luibheid and Norman Russell, trans. (New York: Paulist Press, 1982).

34   "Apophatic theology" is also termed "negative theology," *negative* in that nothing humanly conceivable can adequately define an inexhaustible and illimitable God. The Deity may therefore be conceived as being "unknowable," "hidden," as he was to Moses on Sinai, or as the prophet Isaiah describes him, "Truly, thou art a God who hides himself, O Lord of Israel, the Savior" (45.15). Likewise, when Jesus manifested his glory at the Transfiguration, he radiated a dazzling light "that shone like the sun," a near-blinding brilliance in which he was "hidden." Apophaticism emphasizes contemplative rest in the divine presence, a pure trust beyond human understanding. For more on this topic, see Andrew Louth, *The Origin of the Christian Mystical Tradition* (London: Oxford University Press, 1981) and Louis Bouyer, *The Christian Mystery* (Petersham: St. Bede's Publications, 1995). See also William Johnston, *The Still Point: Reflections on Zen and Christian Mysticism* (New York: Fordham University Press, 1989), for Eastern and Western approaches to God (or "Ultimate Reality") as Eternal and Supreme Mystery.

35   Robert Lax, *Dialogues* (Zurich: Pendo-Verlag, 1994), 81.

36   A Sufi belief has it that a man is not "born" until a mentor-sage helps him to discover inner illumination. Hence the Sufi philosopher Bayezid Bistami (ninth century) states: "When someone asks you how old you are, your reply should not be based on your birth date, but on how many years have transpired since you were truly enlightened." (*Traveling the Path of Love: Sayings of Sufi Masters.* L. Vaughan-Lee, ed. Inverness, California: Golden Sufi Center, 1995, 165). And in Tibetan Buddhism, the importance of acquiring a mentor is great because a sage's counsel helps to speed the time leading to enlightenment. Speed is necessary, since the chance to be reborn in the *human* condition, (and thus possess the capacity to enter Nirvana), is extremely rare. As a popular Tibetan proverb has it, "To be born a human being is as difficult as throwing a six in dice five million times in succession."

37   Simone Weil, *Waiting for God.* E. Craufurd, trans. (New York: HarperCollins, 1973), 58.

38   Another synchronous event relating to my mother and the publication of *Mystic Street* took place when I received the proofs of this book. The FedEx man asked me, "Are you related to Anastasia Georgiou?" After learning she was my mother, he smiled and said, "She's also my daughter's home-school teacher."

39   Rilke, *Letters to a Young Poet* (New York: Vintage, 1986).

40   Or, as Pascal himself put it, "It is the Heart which perceives God, and not the Reason, for all of our reasoning comes down to a surrendering to feeling. The Heart has its reasons of which Reason knows nothing." *Pensées.* A.J. Krailsheimer, trans. (Middlesex: Penguin Books, 1966), 154, 216.

41   Many mystics, such as St. Francis of Assisi, St. John of the Cross, and Blaise Pascal, ultimately spoke of God as being a "Mystery of Love"; as such, God's creation can only wait upon him in love, trusting in divine mercy and grace. Reason goes so far, and then the believer must take a "leap of faith." Likewise, scholarship, even theological scholarship, fades in the Mystery of Love; what the mind can no longer comprehend, the heart may infinitely embrace. A popular example of this concerns Thomas Aquinas, the "Angelic Doctor" who wrote encyclopedic-length works on metaphysics and theology. Shortly before his death, he experienced a mystical revelation that led him to say that his prodigious writings seemed "like so much straw" in comparison to what had been supernaturally revealed to him. Certainly every believer who embraces and participates in this Divine Mystery may be generally deemed a "mystic"; faith issues from the intuitive heart, the very locus of faith, and the source point of mystic revelation.

42   *The Origin and Meaning of Hasidism.* Maurice Friedman, ed. and trans. (New York: Horizon, 1960), 181.

43   From *Not of This World: A Treasury of Christian Mysticism.* J.S. Cutsinger, ed. (Bloomington, IN: World Wisdom, Inc., 2003), 129.

44   Merton. *Conjectures of a Guilty Bystander* (New York: Doubleday, 1968), 157. Like many mystics, Merton intuitively understood that everything is charged with the compassionate energy of God. All things are sustained through the Creator's almighty and unconditional love, without which nothing could exist. It is this Agape that mystics intui-

tively feel, especially in moments of rapture; they see the fire of God's heart everywhere, radiating out of everything.

45   *Artur Schnabel: My Life and Music.* Edward Crankshaw, ed. (New York: St. Martin's Press, 1963).

46   *Bhagavad-Gita.* Barbara Miller, trans. (New York: Bantam, 1986), 151. Meaning "Song of God," the *Bhagavad-Gita* is essentially a compendium of the entire Hindu tradition.

47   On John Main, O.S.B., see *John Main: A Biography in Text and Photos,* by Paul Harris (Catalina, AZ: Medio Media, 2001). See also The World Community for Christian Meditation (www.wccm.org).

48   See *When Prophecy Still Had a Voice: The Collected Letters of Thomas Merton and Robert Lax.* Arthur Biddle, ed. (Lexington, KY: University Press of Kentucky, 2001), 428–429.

49   Yet another serendipitous Laxian occurrence. As *Mystic Street* was going to press, I gave an evening talk on Robert Lax at St. Joseph's Basilica in Alameda, California (an island community near the Berkeley-Oakland area). After I played a recording of Lax reading his poem "A Song for Our Lady," the Poet Laureate of Alameda, Mary Rudge, rose to give the concluding remarks. She had brought with her a March 1957 issue of *Jubilee,* a magazine that contained a poem by Lax that she had planned to read. But of all the "Laxian literature" she could have chosen to recite, Rudge had chosen the very poem that Lax had just read via tape recorder! Once more, Lax made his presence known, this time effecting a connection with someone who, like himself, bore the title "island poet." Interestingly, I had titled the evening's presentation "Island to Island."

50   Thomas Merton, *The Seven Storey Mountain* (New York: Harcourt Brace, 1948), 207–208.

51   *Selected Letters of Jack Kerouac 1940–1956* (January 9, 1951). Ann Charters, ed. (New York: Penguin Books, 1996), 287.

52   Huston Smith, *The Soul of Christianity* (San Francisco: HarperSanFrancisco, 2005).

53   "Texts for the Monks in India," from the *Philokalia*. Palmer-Sherrard-Ware, eds., Vol. 1 (London: Faber and Faber, 1979), 318.

54   For a detailed account of his life, see *Elder Amphilochius Makris: A Contemporary Personality of Patmos*, by Archimandrite Paul Nikitaras. (Patmos: Monastery of St. John Publications, 1990). See also *Our Elder: The Life and Miracles of the Late Amphilochius Makris* (Kalymnos: Holy Monastery of Panaghia Eleousa Publications, 1995).

55   Georgiou, *The Way of the Dreamcatcher*, 222.

56   For more on these hagiographic traditions, see Sr. Nectaria McLees, *Evlogeite! A Pilgrim's Guide to Greece* (Marysville, MO: St. Nicholas Press, 2002).

57   Pascal. *Pensées*. A.J. Krailsheimer, trans. (Middlesex: Penguin Books, 1966), 85.

58   For more on this topic, see George Williams, *Wilderness and Paradise in Christian Thought* (New York: Harper and Row, 1960) and I.A. Bradley, *God Is Green: Christianity and the Environment* (London: Darton, Longman, and Todd, 1990).

59   *The San Francisco Chronicle*, December 14, 2005.

60   Researchers have discovered that when whale sounds are digitally processed, they form precise mandala-like images that are unique to each species. The repetitions in whale songs may follow grammatical rules similar to those of human language, yet another indication of this animal's profound intelligence. See www.aguasonic.com.

61   Isaac of Nineveh. *On Ascetic Life*. Mary Hansbury, trans. (New York: St. Vladimir's Seminary Press, 1989), 12.

62   On Lax and dream communication, see Georgiou, *The Way of the Dreamcatcher*. 58–60, 228.

63   Merton, *Circular Letter to Friends*, September, 1968.

64   Georgiou, *The Way of the Dreamcatcher*, 199.

65   Augustine, *City of God*. G. Walsh, S.J., trans. (New York: Image, 1958), Book 22, 528.

66   Lax, *Journal D*. (Zurich: Pendo-Verlag, 1993), 54–57.

67   Lax, *Notes* (Zurich: Pendo-Verlag, 1995), 90.

68   "Oceans," translated by Robert Bly. From *Written in the Language of the Heart: An Anthology*, by Rick and Louise Nelson (Private Press–Brody's Books, 2002).

69   Augustine, *Confessions*. R.S. Pine-Coffin, trans. (Middlesex: Penguin Books, 1966), 95.

70   Pascal, *Pensées*, 95.

71   *Wisdom of the Native Americans*. K. Nerburn, ed. (Novato, CA: New World Library, 1999), 199.

72   Lax, *Journal C*. (Zurich: Pendo-Verlag, 1990), 66.

73   This early Hebrew idea of resurrection seen in Ezekiel 36.6 (which prefigures the Christian concept of a general resurrection for all) is distinctly physical—the flesh, along with the spirit, rises from the dead. This is again seen in the resurrection of Lazarus (John 11) and in Jesus' resurrection as well (John 20). That both spirit and body rise and partake of a new dimension demonstrates a profound organic spirituality, distinct from many religions of the time, which professed a purely spiritual resurrection. A somatic resurrection indicates that nothing of creation will be lost; all things flowing from the Source of life are holy, since the Source itself is Supreme Holiness. Additionally, if Jesus promises the transformation of this present realm into "a new heaven and a new earth" (Revelation 21), it would stand to reason that humankind would also inherit a "new body" whose somatic make-up would, in some way, hearken of the original paradise. The "macrocosm" and "microcosm" remain ever-bound in the infinite wholeness and sanctity of God. Seen in this light, the "New Eden" (and the glorified bodies of the resurrected) will, in part, issue from the transfigured essence of the original cosmos.

74   *The Way of the Dreamcatcher*, 245.

75   Courtesy of Robert Lax Archives, St. Bonaventure University, New York.

76   Lax, "Port City: The Marseilles Diaries," from *Love Had a Compass*. James Eubbing, ed. (New York: Grove Press, 1996), 191.

77   For more on relics, see T.L. Frazier. *Holy Relics: The Scriptural and Historical Basis for the Veneration of Relics of the Saints* (Ben Lomond, CA: Conciliar Press, 1997).

78   Lax, "Circus of the Sun." From *33 Poems*. Thomas Kellien, ed. (New York: New Directions, 1988), 45.

79   *Mary and the Fathers of the Church: The Blessed Virgin Mary in Patristic Thought*. Luigi Gambaro, ed. Thomas Buffer, trans. (San Francisco: Ignatius Press, 1999), 374.

80   Merton, *The Seven Storey Mountain*, 181.

81   Jack Kerouac: *The Selected Letters 1957–1969*. Ann Charters, ed. (New York: Penguin Books, 1999), 321.

82   This way of self-surrender and egoless inner stillness may be seen in many Christian mystical traditions. Examples include Eastern Orthodox Hesychasm (which advocates a prayerful descent into the "quiet of the heart" in order to better experience the Holy Spirit at work in oneself and the cosmos), fourteenth-century English mysticism (perhaps best represented by the anonymous work, *The Cloud of Unknowing*, a contemplative guide describing how God is approached through the stillness of the heart), the Quietism of seventeenth-century Spain, and Quaker spirituality, with its focus on the wordless serenity of the Inner Light. See Wayne Teasdale, *The Mystic Heart* (Novato, CA: New World Library, 2001).

83   Thomas Merton. *The Seven Storey Mountain* (New York: Harcourt-Brace, 1948), 181.

84   Dr. Mahanambrato Brahmachari arrived penniless in America in 1933, sent by his monastery (Sri Agnan, near Calcutta) to attend the International Conference on the World Fellowship of Faiths in Chicago. His trust in divine grace, that God would take care of him in any situation, gave him the fortitude to live and teach in America from 1933 to 1939. Lax and Merton had heard of this "yellow turbaned and blue sneakered monk" through Sy Freedgood, a mutual college friend. As

Merton describes in *The Seven Storey Mountain*, when Brahmachari came to New York and visited Columbia University, the money-less ascetic needed a place to live, so for a few months he resided in Lax's dormitory room. For more on Brahmachari, see *The Way of the Dreamcatcher*, 71–72, 105.

[85]   Robert Lax, *The Peacemaker's Handbook* (Zurich: Pendo-Verlag, 2001).

[86]   Thomas Merton, *The Way of Chuang Tzu* (Boston: Shambhala, 1992), 158.

[87]   For more on ecospirituality, see the works of Thomas Berry, such as *The Dream of the Earth* (San Francisco: Sierra Club Books, 1990). See also *The Last Hours of Ancient Sunlight*, by Thom Hartmann (New York: Three Rivers Press, 2004).

[88]   Excerpt from a letter by Mallarmé to a friend, dated July 16, 1866. From *The Poetics of Space* by Gaston Bachelard (Boston: Beacon Press, 1994), 85.

[89]   Melchizedek appears in Genesis 14.18-20 and Hebrews 7.1-6.

[90]   The belief that every sensitive and conscious individual should function as a "Minister of Nature" is especially emphasized by poet-mystics such as William Wordsworth, and, in particular, Ralph Waldo Emerson and the writers of the American Transcendentalist Movement.

[91]   Simone Weil. *Waiting for God*. E. Craufurd, trans. (New York: HarperCollins Books, 2001), 109–110. Many of the founding Church Fathers, such as Sts. Irenaeus, Ignatius, Basil the Great, Gregory of Nyssa, John Chrysostom, and Gregory Nazianzen also wrote of Christ Incarnate as the supreme "Mystery of the Cosmos" (*Mysterion tou Kosmou*). Later Orthodox theologians (St. Maximus the Confessor and St. Simeon the New Theologian) strongly emphasize this theme.

[92]   Most mystics accentuate the need to "wait on God." Contact with the Deity (and divine revelation) cannot be humanly engineered; both must come down from heaven, and in heaven's own good time. To do otherwise would be to display *hubris*, and, in essence, "force the issue." Hence, so many pre-Christian myths and biblical stories emphasize how

pride (and a relentlessly headstrong and self-centred attitude) can lead to destruction. This theme is exhibited in the familiar Tower of Babel story, (Genesis 11.1-9), in which a tower was straightaway built from earth to heaven, an overbold attempt, perhaps, to make contact with the Divine (hence God's thwarting of this grandiose scheme). Eventually, however, the Divinity reaches out to humankind, that creation might indeed enter heaven through the Christ, the "Tower" uniting this life with the next. Thus all things come to be fulfilled through "waiting on God" via faith, hope, patience, and love.

[93]   Lax, *Psalm* (Zurich: Pendo-Verlag, 1991), 10, 20.

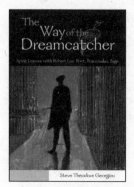

Praise for Steve Georgiou's
The Way of the Dreamcatcher

"Unpretentious, thoughtful, refreshing, this is a gem of a book. The book's true subject is holiness."

—Kathleen Norris, author of *The Cloister Walk* and *Amazing Grace*

"Precisely a book to give to a friend."

—Sr. Renee Brannigan, O.S.B. *American Monastic Review*

"Joyful tranquility flows from the pages of this book. Here Lax emerges as a Gandalf-like figure who has found refuge on a quiet island off the shore of Middle Earth."

—Jim Forest, founder of the Orthodox Peace Fellowship

"This warm, inspiring text allows the reader to learn and laugh with a man numerous authors have affectionately termed 'a saint'."

—Brother Patrick Hart, O.C.S.O., Abbey of Gethsemani

"Georgiou has provided us with a very full and connected portrait of Lax as no one has before."

—Paul Spaeth, Director, Lax Archives, St. Bonaventure University

"The engaging dialogue between Lax and Georgiou opens up a new world of spiritual wisdom that is at once simple and sublime; this book breathes a sense of God's presence."

—Monsignor William Shannon, founder of the International Thomas Merton Society

"Anyone interested in exploring the mind of a poet and mystic will find this a fascinating read."

—Clare Boehmer, *Review for Religious*

"The real deal—this book offers readers the rare opportunity to experience the humility, clarity, and spiritual insight of a man whom Jack Kerouac called 'The Laughing Buddha.'"

—George Wallace, *Poetrybay Review*

"From Georgiou's work, it is obvious that even sixty years on, it was the friendship equally with the faith and poetry that had sustained Lax."

—Arthur Jones, *National Catholic Reporter*

"The Way of the Dreamcatcher is a creation of love."

—Rosemary Radford Ruether, author of *Mary: The Feminine Face of the Church*

"This book captures the essence of one of the twentieth century's enlightened beings, the poet and contemplative Robert Lax. It gives access to the wisdom and humor of a thinker and writer who deserves to be much better known."

—Arthur Biddle, editor of *When Prophecy Still Had a Voice: The Collected Letters of Thomas Merton and Robert Lax*

"The Way of the Dreamcatcher will be cherished for its radiance of spirit."

—*The Prairie Messenger*

"This book enables Lax to continue sharing his wisdom with readers, poets, priests, and artists who strive to bring good to the world."

—*Nimble Spirit: The Literary Spirituality Review*

"A book of visions... The symbols that Georgiou and Lax share will bear fruition for eternity."

—D.K. Phillips, editor of *Thomas Merton: Monk and Poet*

"Anybody who reads this book will be inspired."

—Jonathan Carr, *Athens News*, Greece

"A storehouse of treasure. Read this book, especially if you are a writer, artist, poet, mentor, or spiritual director."

—Paul Fromont, *Prodigal Kiwi*, New Zealand

"This is a powerful work. It emphasizes Christ's message of having a peaceful and loving heart that flows to those around us."

—Michael Shackleton, *The Southern Cross*, South Africa's National Catholic Weekly

"Living like a lay monastic on the 'Isle of the Apocalypse,' Lax meditates on the meaning of life and uplifts us with the richness of his words."

—Fr. Anthony Coniaris, Light & Life Orthodox Press

"A fascinating portrait of the 'Poet of Patmos.' Recommended as a personal testimony to an outstanding human being."

—Charles Cummings, O.C.S.O. *Cistercian Studies Quarterly*

"Contains nuggets of wisdom."

—*The Toronto Star*

"A valuable contribution to Merton Studies."

—Gregory Kilcourse, *The Merton Annual*

"A poignant and down-to-earth read for anybody who is searching."

—Jonathon Montaldo, The Merton Institute for Contemplative Living

"Those seeking a perfect example of life lived in true love, a life that brought out the best in others, would enjoy reading this volume immensely."

—Jack Kelly, *The Acorn: A Journal of the Gandhi-King Society*

"Heartwarming; a return to simplicity."

—*Beat Scene Magazine*, London

"A marvelous book of blessing with a strong power to inspire, amuse, entertain."

—Monsignor G.T. Fehily, Christian Meditation Centre, Dublin, Ireland

"A useable guide for those seeking their own way to holiness."

—Wade Hall, *The Courier Journal*

"Such a joy to read!"

—Fernando Beltran Llavador, International Thomas Merton Society, Spain

"Reading this book is like a breath of fresh air."

—Angus Stuart, International Thomas Merton Society, England

"In this powerful text, Lax reveals the fruits of his spiritual and creative life. His story demonstrates how life in the Spirit has no boundaries. He shows us what is possible when we make the Heart our centre."

—Detlev Cuntz, International Thomas Merton Society, Germany

"To be read over and over again."

—*The Hellenic Journal*, San Francisco

"Robert Lax lives in this book!"

—Simone Landrien, L'Arche, Trosly, France

"Through his luminous interplay with Robert Lax, Georgiou has painted a loving portait of a remarkable human being. A doorway to a man who deserves much attention has been opened."

—Peter Maravelis, City Lights Books, San Francisco

"To read this book is to listen in to a long, heartfelt conversation between one who is wise and one who seeks wisdom. The subject is the most difficult and most necessary thing in the world—*intentional love*, that is, the love that transcends all desire for pleasure or personal gain. And we put the book down understanding that to develop the capacity for such love is what we human beings are here for."

—Jacob Needleman, author of *Why Can't We Be Good?* and *Lost Christianity*